Down For His Crimes

by Evan Jacobs

D1568874

Ronni's Books/Anhedenia Films

Other Books by Evan Jacobs

My Summer of Hate
JD
Screaming Quietly

For my parents
My brother
Shawn Miller and Family
IB and the "cast" of Room D12
and the student "from a long time ago"

Chapter 1.

Seeker's eyes got wide when he saw Mr. Setari. They hadn't seen each other since Seeker was in Third grade. He'd been a little kid then. Seeker was an Eighth grader now. It was between classes. Seeker was supposed to be in Intervention. It was for students who were in danger of failing a class (or classes). Seeker wasn't in danger of failing anything; he just needed help with math. He didn't mind being in there, though. That's where most of his friends were.

Before he knew what was happening, Seeker and Mr. Setari shook hands. Instinctively, Seeker gave him hug; just like he had in Third grade.

And then, as quickly as that happened, Seeker pulled away. He looked around to see if anybody else had seen him hugging a teacher. Nobody was around.

"You're here now?" Seeker asked.

School had started a few weeks ago.

"Yeah," Mr. Setari beamed. "How you doing Sergio? Its been a long time. You still drawing?"

Seeker nodded his head and started to move away from him. Even though he was older, Mr. Setari looked the same. He still had slicked back brown hair and wore adult clothes like sweaters and button up shirts.

"It's great to see you." Mr. Setari continued.

"I've got Intervention." Seeker pointed in the direction of the Intervention room he needed to go to.

"Alright." Mr. Setari continued to smile at him. "We'll talk later. Take care of what you need to take care of, Sergio."

"Cool."

Seeker was walking away before the word left his mouth. He increased his pace so that Mr. Setari wouldn't talk to him anymore. So he wouldn't call him Sergio anymore. Nobody called Seeker by his real name, Sergio Torres. At least nobody that really knew him.

It hadn't always been like this.

In Third Grade Seeker thought Mr. Setari was awesome. He was fun and he brought toys to class. He had a lot of energy. He hadn't been the teacher of the class. Mr. Setari just worked in it as aide and he made it fun. Seeker loved going to school then.

Now?

School was just a place that he went to in-between hanging out with his friends. He didn't hate it. It was just whatever.

Seeker didn't know when he started to look at school that way. It just seemed like something that happened as he got older.

When he was almost at the Intervention room, Seeker looked back to see if Mr. Setari was watching him. He wasn't. Seeker knew he wouldn't be. He felt stupid for even looking.

That didn't mean Seeker was going to give him any more hugs. He was too old for that stuff now. He used to give a lot of people hugs when he was younger. Not anymore.

Chapter 2.

"Alright! Two minutes!" Mr. Robert's voice bellowed. He was the school security guard. Mr. Robert was a big guy with black, slick backed hair and a goatee. The students had two minutes to get from class to class. If they didn't make it, they'd better hope they could get there before Mr. Robert saw them.

Mr. Robert was tough and he could be mean. Seeker had never had any problems with him, but that was because Mr. Robert always seemed to be one step ahead. In fact, he'd laugh when Seeker would try to push the two minute mark to its absolute limit. He'd clown him about it and Seeker was quick enough to keep up with the insults. He knew he was better off just going to class.

Hector Munoz had crossed Mr. Robert before. And Mr. Fry, the Principal. Hector was Seeker's best friend and the leader of their gang.

The Little Killerz.

They hadn't ever killed anyone. They just jumped a few people, stole things from the store... nothing big. Nothing that would make The Little Killerz targets of the cops like the bigger gangs 11th Street or the Owen Street Creepers.

Hector had been fighting ever since he and Seeker met in kindergarten. He was tall and had black hair that was shaved down. He had eyes that always looked angry. Hector had a short temper with everybody.

Adults, kids... it didn't matter.

If you mad dogged or talked in a way Hector thought was dissing him, he'd throw punches and ask questions later. He had mellowed a bit since he'd gotten older, but not much.

As Seeker walked with Hector, he put his arm around his girlfriend, Angel Carrillo. They'd been going out for almost a month. They'd been friends since Fifth grade. Seeker liked

Angel a lot. She had a long black hair, dark skin and always wore skimpy clothes that revealed her blossoming body. Seeker thought she was beautiful.

They passed Anthony, Irvin and Nathan. They all shook hands and walked together even though they didn't have the same class.

Anthony had big curly hair and usually wore the same clothes; a big green hoodie and jeans. Irvin was short and always wore video game t-shirts. Nathan seemed to wear clothes that were hand-me-downs from his brother. Usually jeans and shirts for punk bands like Cro-Mags, Sick of It All or Black Flag.

These were The Little Killerz.

Principal Fry was a bald, stocky man who always wore a button shirt and a tie. He was alright. Seeker had gotten in trouble for mouthing off in class once. He'd also gotten in trouble for ditching school or being out of class when he shouldn't have been. Principal Fry was cool to him. Seeker didn't even get in that much trouble.

There was a vice principal and another security guard but Seeker didn't know them that well.

The bell rang.

Seeker and Angel kissed and he casually walked off to class.

Chapter 3.

"You're gonna kick his ass, Hector. It's gonna be so gangster." Anthony and Hector shook hands after he said that.

Seeker, Hector, Anthony, Irvin and Nathan were walking down the street after school. They were carrying their backpacks. They were on their way to a fight. It was between Hector and Javier Rosas.

"It probably won't stay between them." Seeker thought.

Javier was supposed to graduate to Ninth Grade this year but he got held back. As a result he looked bigger than all the students on campus. He was the leader of the Owen Street Hoods. They were the younger version of the Owen Street Creepers. Eventually they'd become full fledged Hoods.

"He won't talk about you anymore after this." Irvin offered Hector.

Seeker was waiting for Nathan to say something. Hector liked being given ego boosts from these guys. Seeker figured that was probably why he liked having them around.

He respected Hector. Seeker knew him the best. He had been over to his house. He'd seen his mom yell at him and his dad (and brothers) beat him up. Seeker knew him too well to kiss his butt.

"He isn't gonna say anything after this." Hector glared. "Javier didn't think what he said would get back to me but it did and now I'm gonna mess him up."

Javier had made some comment about Hector. They had been friends in elementary school. This was before Seeker and Hector started to hang out. Then one day they got mad at each other. Then they started fighting. Things never got made right. Javier was now Hector's mortal enemy.

After that Seeker and Hector became best friends.

Whenever Hector and the Little Killerz fought anybody it was always the same thing. Somebody had been talking smack about Hector and it got back to him. Seeker wouldn't have minded fighting if they were fighting for something. They were just fighting because Hector had a lot of enemies.

He also had a lot of friends too. That made him somebody whose good side you wanted to be on.

Hector was always telling the Little Killerz that they had to fight. If they didn't fight the other gangs would think they were weak. Hector told them that if they fought enough, if they stole enough, they could make a name for themselves. Eventually, they would get bigger, more members, and the Little Killerz would rule.

Seeker looked at the walls as they walked. He'd much rather be painting right now. He loved to draw and create graffiti art. Seeker knew that a lot of people didn't want him marking up their buildings. He always tried to do it in places that not a lot of people could see. This way people would have to "seek" it out. Like he was Batman or Iron Man or another superhero from one of those movies he loved so much.

Sergio "Seeker" Torres was an artist for all who sought him.

It took him awhile to realize that he was following after Hector, Anthony, Irvin and Nathan now. Seeker was doing this more and more when they walked together. All the guys tried to walk with Hector.

"To be cool. To be seen." Seeker told himself. He didn't really care.

At the same time, he didn't want to be too far behind the Little Killerz.

Chapter 4.

Seeker stood a few feet behind Hector.

Anthony, Irvin and Nathan were standing a few feet behind them clustered in a group. Hector figured if anybody else came at him while he was fighting Javier, the other guys could stop them.

They were in an industrial area. It was mostly businesses that we're no longer in business. A lot of homeless people hung out there and they wouldn't care if a bunch of young kids were fighting.

"This would be a cool spot to hit." Seeker thought, imagining how his tags might look there.

Javier stood across from Hector. They were about two feet from each other. Javier only had a few members of the Owen Street Hoods with him.

Seeker got a sick feeling when he saw this. He knew that there were way more members than he was seeing.

"Why you gotta say that stuff?" Hector asked. "Tryin' to be all big time?"

Hector and Javier had been going back and forth about who said what about whom.

"You're all hurt about what I said why don't you do something about it?" Javier was calm and cool. He had a shaved head too. He was taller and more muscular than Hector. He wore a black shirt and baggy, black jeans. The other members of the Owen Street Hoods were dressed pretty much the same way.

"That's why I'm here." Hector smiled. "I told everybody I'd beat your ass. You don't see me running."

"Try it then." Javier's eyes were wide.

This was always the tensest time. Right before the rumble was really getting started. Right before somebody just took control (or lost it) and threw the first punch.

Javier must not have fought Hector in a long time. He must've forgotten how quick Hector was.

Hector was tough and he was angry. And when he fought he exploded.

He landed two really clean punches on Javier. Before Javier fell down, Hector grabbed him and hit him again.

Javier's body dropped to the ground.

The other members of the Owen Street Hoods started to push Seeker and the other Little Killerz. Before Seeker knew what was happening, he was grappling with somebody and throwing punches at them.

Whoever he was fighting managed to land a bunch of looping punches on Seeker. He felt them bounce off his head and shoulders. Seeker was taller and he managed to pull the person down and knee him a bunch of times in the crotch in stomach.

"Ugh..." He heard him moan.

Seeker, completely in fight mode now, brought this nameless person he didn't know up and slugged him in the face. His foe fell back and then ran away.

He looked around and saw that Anthony, Irvin and Nathan were also beating up the people they were fighting.

"Little Killerz!!" Seeker yelled out.

Seeker looked over and saw Hector. He was smiling a prideful smile at his friend. They had known each other a long time. Hector knew he could trust Seeker. He knew he was down for his crimes.

Seeker smiled back and looked around. The guys that Anthony, Nathan and Irvin had been fighting were also running away.

"You better run!" Javier yelled at them.

That's when Seeker noticed that members of the Owen Street Creepers were showing up.

Chapter 5.

It soon became clear to Seeker that this had been a set-up. Javier had probably told some of the members of Owen Street about the Littler Killerz. He probably figured it would make him look good to the Creepers if they could stomp out the Little Killerz before they got too big.

"Bail!!" Hector yelled as more members of Owen Street circled them.

Seeker and Javier took off with Anthony, Irvin and Nathan far behind.

Seeker knew that if any one of them got caught they all got caught. You couldn't leave your friend to take a beating for all of you.

"Come on," Seeker told himself about the others. "Keep up."

The buildings in the industrial area led out to a busy street. If they made it out there the Little Killerz could get away easier. That was if there weren't more members of Owen Street waiting.

Hector and Seeker made it out onto the street. Seeker glanced back and saw that Anthony, Irvin and Nathan had made it as well. His fears that Owen Street would have a bunch of people waiting, staked out to get them, never happened.

About a mile away from where the fight had taken place, the Little Killerz stopped running.

Chapter 6.

"You totally stomped him, Hector. That was way gangster!" Irvin beamed as they ate at Taco Bell. They all had more money than normal that day.

"He didn't even get to land a punch." Anthony offered.

"I kicked my guy's ass." Nathan said.

Hector ate his burrito and fries. He just nodded his head. As if it was a foregone conclusion that if Hector fought somebody, he'd beat them easily.

Seeker had been seeing Hector fight forever. He fought so well Seeker had probably had less fights because of him. As Seeker sipped his cherry coke he tried to remember a fight that Hector had lost. He couldn't.

"They almost ambushed us." Seeker said. He wasn't trying to bring everybody down.

"If Hector's such a good fighter, such a good leader, how could he lead the Little Killerz into an ambush?" He wondered.

He didn't dare say that. Hector would get mad and then Seeker would probably have to fight him. Seeker wasn't scared of Hector but he didn't want to be on his bad side.

Like Javier. Like everybody who wasn't down for Hector.

"They needed all those guys to try and beat us." Irvin said.

"Yeah, we're just a small set. We took on Owen Street and basically beat them. Imagine what we could do if we had more back up? We'd be way more gangster." Hector looked around the table as he talked.

"That'd be rad." Irvin smiled. He was totally down for Hector.

"Hector could tell him to rob his mom and he'd do it." Seeker thought.

He took out a pen and drew on a napkin.

Seeker wished that was what he'd done that afternoon. Painting.

Instead he'd been in a fight. He didn't regret it. He just got antsy when he didn't create for awhile. Seeker used to get in trouble in class because he'd draw when the other kids were taking notes.

Principal Fry thought the drawing might be helping him. So they had Seeker take a quiz after he'd been "doodling" during his history class. He got a high B. None of the teachers at Cutter Middle School ever bothered him about drawing in class again.

The conversation about the future of the Little Killerz continued. Seeker was paying attention even though Hector might've thought he wasn't.

Chapter 7.

As Seeker walked home he saw a STOP sign in the distance. Out of instinct he quickly pulled a black marker out of his pocket. He did it so quickly and concealed it with his hand so well; nobody would ever know that he had it.

He looked around. Seeker didn't see any cars coming up or down the street. There was nobody walking around except for an old lady with her dog. Some kids were playing basketball at a nearby park but none of them would notice him.

In Seeker's mind he was like Spider-Man or The Dark Knight. He worked quick and skillfully. By the time he got done, by the time anybody realized what was going on, Seeker was gone.

On to his next painting. His next tag.

Seeker may not have been stopping crime but he wasn't hurting anybody either. He just wanted to spread his name. To let people know that there was somebody creating around them. Somebody who was making something. Seeking something.

As he approached the sign he flipped the cap off the marker into his other hand. Then he went to work.

When Seeker did this it was as if his hands became disconnected from his body. He wrote his name.

SeekeR.

The S was big and the R was big. For some reason he thought that this would get people's attention. Make him more visible and more of a mystery at the same time.

He didn't look at anything. Not the people playing basketball, not the old lady walking her dog across the street, not even the white letters that spelled STOP on the sign.

The stroke of his black marker moved in jagged lines along the red paint of the sign. It was as if Seeker was building something from the ground up.

What he loved about graffiti was that it was cheap and he could do it anywhere. All he needed was a marker or some paint and he could create something. The whole neighborhood was his canvas.

And then, just as quickly as he started, Seeker was done.

He capped the marker and discretely walked away from the stop sign. He put the marker in his pocket.

Seeker looked around a little bit as he went. He didn't want to walk too quickly and he didn't want to look around too much. Most of all Seeker didn't want to look guilty. Then he spotted Mr. Setari driving down the street.

At first, he hadn't seen Seeker. Seeker just stared at him for too long. Mr. Setari turned and saw him. He smiled at Seeker and waved. Seeker almost waved back.

But he didn't.

Seeker quickly turned his head and looked the other way. He hoped Mr. Setari hadn't really noticed him. He didn't want to be mean. Seeker didn't have anything against him. He just couldn't be friends with a teacher.

The principal, Mr. Robert, they were different. All the students had to deal with them.

Seeker didn't want to deal with anybody he didn't have to. His life was complicated enough.

Chapter 8.

"You broke it!" Pablo, Seeker's 6 year old nephew, said to Roman. Roman was Seeker's 4 year old nephew. They were Isabel's kids. Isabel was Seeker's older sister.

Seeker was in the bedroom he shared with them trying to read a history lesson. He liked reading and he thought history was cool. He especially liked learning about the Mayans and the Aztecs. That's not what he was reading about tonight. Seeker was studying the colonies and how the US was founded. It was alright. There hadn't been any wars yet. Or any battles with Native Americans. The people that had come to the US were just suffering.

"Go somewhere else!" Seeker said to his nephews without looking up from his book.

"This is our room too!" Pablo snapped back.

"Then be quiet." Seeker glared at him. "I'm trying to read." He would've gone into the living room but Mario, his sister's boyfriend was in there.

Mario was cool. He didn't bug Seeker about anything. Seeker's only problem with Mario (if Mario was staying at the apartment they all shared), was that he was always in the living room. If he wasn't playing video games he was watching TV. No matter what he did in there, it was always loud and Seeker couldn't concentrate.

Sometimes Mario and Isabel would get into a fight and Mario would stay other places for weeks; sometimes months. Seeker wondered if he was ever going to marry his sister and move out. He figured that Mario probably wouldn't. He had a good set-up. Seeker's dad let them stay there rent free. His dad didn't get involved with any of them really.

Seeker's dad was hardly ever at home when everybody was around. He worked as a maintenance man for a school. As far back as Seeker could remember he'd always done that. His dad drank a little but not that much.

Not as much as Mario. He liked beer. Mario would also go into the small backyard of their apartment and smoke pot. Mario had offered Seeker some of both. Seeker drank a little beer but he stayed away from pot. He thought it smelled gross. He didn't tell Hector or the other guys that. They wouldn't understand.

Seeker's mom had died of cancer six years before. Ever since then his dad stopped being a dad. He provided the house and some food. After work he liked to hang out with his friends and play cards. Sometimes they did it at Seeker's house but most of the time his dad went elsewhere.

Isabel got Seeker clothes here and there. He basically only wore a few different shirts, hoodies and pairs of jeans. He always had holes in his socks. Isabel also paid for Seeker's cell phone.

Eventually, Seeker's nephews got bored and they left the room. This allowed Seeker to concentrate.

As he read about the first settlers in America, he sort of related to them not having much. The apartment he lived in had three bedrooms. Seeker shared one with his nephews. Isabel and Mario stayed in another one. His dad had one to himself.

Almost all the apartments in the neighborhood were like that: Packed with people who didn't have a lot of money. There were kid's toys and trash all over the place, one park with almost nothing in it for all the kids to use, screen doors painted white so that nobody could look inside and see what anybody else had, etc. Still, despite all of this, in Seeker's neighborhood there was a sense of community. Everybody knew one another. If somebody needed help the neighbors did their best to give it. There were still fights but Seeker wasn't scared of the people he lived around.

He just wanted more space.

"To not have to be in a gang and be hard."

Seeker wanted to be free.

He knew his life wasn't nearly as tough as the early settlers he was reading about. Seeker also knew that they created something pretty incredible from almost nothing.

If they could do that he figured he could do something with what he had; his gift.

Painting.

Graffiti.

Chapter 9.

"When did you start going by the name Seeker?" Mr. Setari asked.

When he'd first come up to him Seeker thought that Mr. Setari was gonna bust him for tagging his name on the STOP sign the day before. He didn't say anything about it.

"I don't know." Seeker said. He was hoping if he said that enough Mr. Setari might get the hint. Saying "I don't know" usually stopped more questions.

So far it wasn't working.

"How's school going? You psyched about going to high school next year?" Mr. Setari kept coming with the questions.

Seeker nodded his head. He looked around to see if anybody was watching him. It was snack time. Most of the students were in the food area eating or hanging out on the field or blacktop. Seeker had less than 15 minutes to eat and he was starving. He hadn't even bought his food yet and he was sure there was going to be a line.

"I hear you're still drawing." Mr. Setari continued. He'd obviously been talking to people about Seeker. Telling him that he'd known Seeker for awhile. Seeker just hoped he wasn't telling other students.

"Yeah, I like drawing." Seeker had to say something. "I don't know," "Yeah" and nodding his head just wasn't enough of a hint to Mr. Setari that he didn't want to talk. Seeker didn't know what he was gonna do. He couldn't be rude, though. Mr. Setari was still a teacher. Seeker didn't want to get in trouble.

Seeker saw some people he knew. They didn't seem to notice he was talking to Mr. Setari.

"I gotta go eat my snack." Seeker finally said. He felt kinda bad but he wasn't lying.

"Sure, no problem. Eat your snack. I'll catch you later." Mr. Setari walked back over to his room.

Seeker gave the students he'd seen the "what's up" nod as he headed toward the snack area.

Chapter 10.

At lunch Seeker and Angel were making out behind the PE building. They'd been looking for Hector and the others, but they'd ended up there. Angel's lips were soft and they tasted like bubble gum because of the lip gloss she was wearing. Her tongue was soft and wet. Seeker always tried to have mints on him because he wanted his breath to smell good. So far, Angel hadn't complained.

He could feel himself getting really worked up with Angel. Her skin was so soft. Her mouth so warm and inviting. She was perfect to him. Angel always looked perfect.

They had gone pretty far but not all the way. Seeker was pretty sure Angel had been all the way a few times. Still, he thought he was special to her because that was the way she made him feel.

Seeker had liked Angel since they first met but she'd always had different boyfriends. He knew at one time that Hector kind of liked her. For some reason it never happened. Hector was the leader of the Little Killerz. Angel seemed to like guys that were in gangs; that were tough. As far as Seeker knew she and Hector never hooked up. Hector may have been too intense for her.

Seeker was kind of worried when they started hanging out that Hector would get mad. Not because he was scared of Hector, he just didn't want to have any problems with him over Angel.

Seeker felt that Angel liked him a lot but he didn't know if she loved him. He was pretty sure he loved her. She didn't seem to care about him outside of the gang and the world of Cutter Middle School, though.

He would draw her things he thought she would like. And she did... but she didn't seem to like them for long. Seeker would give them to her and never see them again.

Eventually, they continued looking for Hector and the rest of the Little Killerz. Seeker was glad. If they'd kept going, kissing and everything, he didn't know if he was going to be able to control himself.

Chapter 11.

At snack the next day Seeker saw a crowd gathering in the open hallway of the school. He didn't see any teachers around so he knew the chances of there being a fight were good.

"Nobody's stupid enough to get in a fight in front of a teacher." Seeker told himself.

As he got closer, Seeker saw that the standoff was between Hector and Javier. This wasn't supposed to happen. There was a sort of agreement that the gangs wouldn't fight at school. It made them too visible to the teachers, school security and the cops.

Seeker immediately pushed his way to the front so he could stand behind Hector. Some of the Owen Street Hoods were behind Javier. People moved out of the way for Seeker. They knew he was supposed to be with Hector.

"We beat your asses and then you had to get more punks!" Hector yelled.

"You're the punks that ran away! Little Killerz more like Little Bitches!!" Javier said. He was inches from Hector's face.

Hector started punching and kicking Javier. Seeker saw the other Owen Street guys trying to grab Hector. He pushed them away so that it could be a fair fight. He thought they might go after him but they didn't. Seeker hoped Anthony, Irvin and Nathan would get over there soon. He knew the other guys from Owen Street would probably be showing up. Then it would be a much bigger fight...

Hector had Javier on the ground again. Hector was kicking him and trying to stomp him on the head. Seeker wanted to grab him and bail.

The Little Killerz had won. No point in sticking around to get in trouble for it.

Suddenly, two hands grabbed Hector and pulled him away from Javier.

It was Mr. Setari.

Chapter 12.

"Get off me!" Hector yelled. He turned around and looked at Mr. Setari like he wanted to kill him.

"What's the problem here, Seeker?" Mr. Setari eyed him.

Seeker didn't know what to say. He didn't want people to think he was actually friends with Mr. Setari. At the same time, if Mr. Setari thought they were friends maybe Seeker could talk him into not taking Hector to the principal.

"He started it!" Javier yelled.

He quickly got up off the ground. Some of the Owen Street Hoods chimed in behind him.

"Shut up!" Hector turned and pushed Javier into them.

Javier just smiled. When Hector lost his temper it was hard for him to come out of it.

"Why don't you just relax?" Mr. Setari said.

Hector glared at him.

"What are you guys fighting about? Whose got the baggier pants?" Mr. Setari smiled. Seeker knew what he was doing. He was giving Hector a chance to fix himself up.

Some of the kids laughed. Hector wasn't one of them. He cursed at Mr. Setari. Seeker moved closer because he thought Hector might try to hit him. He couldn't let that happen.

"Who are you to make fun of my clothes? You think I'm poor?? That my clothes are ghetto and my parents can't buy me new ones???" Hector was screaming now.

"Lets go to the office?" Mr. Setari's expression suddenly changed. All the smiles were gone. His eyes were getting wide. He turned his body and pointed to the office. "Either start walking or I'm gonna have Mr. Robert walk you there."

Mr. Robert walked up behind the crowd of students.

"Everything okay, Mr. Setari? Hector giving you trouble?" He asked. He purposely seemed to be trying not to make any eye contact with Seeker or any of the others. Mr. Robert's tone was hard.

"Yeah, you need Mr. Robert because you're a punk and you can't take me to the principal yourself!" Hector was still furious because he knew he was beat.

"Just keep talking. You're making it a lot more difficult on yourself." Mr. Setari's expression was calm and stern. He may have been willing to cut Hector some slack. Not now. He was gonna let Hector hang himself.

"Punk." Hector walked toward the office. Mr. Setari followed him.

"Mr. Setari?" Mr. Robert called. He motioned toward Seeker, Javier and the other Owen Street Hoods. "What about these guys?"

Both Hector and Mr. Setari looked back.

"They're fine." Mr. Setari said. "This is all Hector."

Seeker shook his head and looked at the ground.

"It's not all Hector," He told himself. "He just made it that way."

Chapter 13.

Somewhere before Seeker's next period PE class he found out that Hector had been suspended for three weeks. As he walked with Anthony and Irvin to PE, a thought suddenly dawned on him.

"I'm in charge of the Little Killerz."

Seeker didn't want that. Even though he didn't look up to Hector the way Anthony, Irvin and Nathan did, Seeker never wanted to be the person fronting the Little Killerz. He liked being the back up. He liked knowing that Hector knew he could count on him. No matter what Seeker was down.

"What if Javier and the other guys in Owen Street started messing with the Little Killerz more now?" Seeker asked himself. "What if I make decisions for the gang that Hector doesn't like? Will I have to fight everybody?"

Seeker didn't want to fight at all. He just wanted to paint on walls. To spread his name everywhere. To be in the shadows like Batman or The Punisher.

"Hey Sergio." A voice said.

Seeker spun around and saw that it was Mr. Setari.

"Hey." Seeker said.

Seeker continued to look at Mr. Setari as he backpedaled.

"How you doing?" Mr. Setari seemed to be talking about something else. He wanted to know how Seeker felt about Hector being suspended.

"Does he think I'm mad at him?" Seeker wondered.

If Seeker hadn't been standing in front of Mr. Setari he would've laughed at the thought.

"An adult would never care if a kid was mad at them." Seeker told himself.

Anthony and Irvin continued walking to PE.

"I'm cool." Seeker replied.

The two minute bell sounded.

Seeker turned and walked away from Mr. Setari.

Mr. Robert could be heard yelling "Two minutes!" from across the school.

Mr. Setari couldn't be mad at Seeker for bailing. He'd get in trouble if he wasn't at PE on time.

Chapter 14.

"I shoulda decked that punk ass teacher." Hector was just as angry at Mr. Setari as he had been hours before.

Seeker was sitting next to Hector in a booth at Del Taco. He was sipping water and drawing his name on a napkin. He was experimenting with not making the lines so jagged. He was going for a bubble look. Seeker found that hard to do with spray paint. He was also wondering what color he would do it in. Seeker wanted it to look like his name was coming out of the water. He didn't know if he could do that with spray paint but he was going to try.

"I wish I woulda been there." Irvin said. "I woulda hit him for you."

Anthony and Irvin were sitting across from them. Nathan had pulled up a chair at the table. Anthony had bought a coke and Nathan had bought fries. They were all sharing them. Each one of them was taking turns going up to the soda fountain and getting a drink with the one cup Anthony bought.

"You weren't there." Seeker eyed Irvin. "Some back up."

None of them said anything. Seeker didn't want to be mean to his friends. He was just tired of all this "Hector Worship." He wished he could go back to when they were kids. When none of them wanted to be hard or tough. When they just wanted to have fun, ride their bikes or skateboards, and just hang around.

Those days weren't completely gone but they almost were.

"I wanna get that teacher." Hector stated. His voice was low. He eyed all the Little Killerz.

"What about Javier?" Nathan asked.

"We can always deal with him." He snapped. "All of you stay down with the Hoods. We don't want to give Fry or anybody else a reason to think we're planning something."

Seeker looked at Anthony, Irvin and Nathan. They all wore the same blank expression. Seeker realized they were all thinking the same thing.

Hector had always been bolder than all of them. He was always the quickest to talk back and throw the first punch.

But going after Mr. Setari? This was a whole new ball game. Not only was he an adult...

He was a teacher.

"What are you gonna do?" Seeker asked.

He may not have wanted to be around Mr. Setari but he didn't want anything bad to happen to him.

"Don't worry." Hector's anger suddenly turned into a smile. It scared Seeker because Hector was so mean and happy at the same time.

"He looks like a demon." Seeker thought.

Hector continued to smile.

"I want you to find out what car he drives. I'm gonna show him if he or anybody else messes with me... or the Little Killerz... they're gonna pay for it."

He took a big drink off the soda.

Seeker looked down at the table.

"What does he want to know Mr. Setari's car for?" Seeker wondered angrily.

Now that Hector was gone, he thought he'd just have to worry about dealing with the Owen Street Hoods at school. Now he had to worry about what Hector was gonna do when he was out of it.

Chapter 15.

Seeker found a wall and began to work on his new tag. He was really taking his time, trying to make his name look like it was emerging out of water. Seeker was using just black and blue spray paint. It was too dark. The blue needed to be lighter.

"This is what's tough about graffiti," he thought. "I want it to look good but when I do it, I've got to do it fast."

This was why he was always stealing time to create. He'd draw on his school work, his notes, toilet paper... he didn't care. Seeker wanted his designs to be perfect. He wanted them to stand out. It was all part of his plan.

He was the Seeker. Always looking for a place to work on his art. To spread his name. Seeker wanted people see his work and say how good it was.

When Seeker painted he was really able to relax. When he first started painting on the street he thought he would be really stressed. That having to put up all those colors into a good looking design would be impossible.

It was never like that.

When Seeker started to paint he was good at it. He'd gotten better over the years. Seeker was all self-taught. He'd grown up seeing tags and people tagging around his neighborhood, but he never knew any of those guys. He just knew that it looked cool to him. Most of them worked with a "point" person. They had them looking out in case the cops or a building owner came by.

Not Seeker.

He liked working alone. Just like his favorite superheroes. When he's painting he's not in a gang, he's not in school, and he doesn't live in a poor neighborhood.

He's not Sergio... he's just Seeker... and that's all he needs to be.

About a year ago he got Nathan to shoot a video of him painting a wall on his phone. Nathan's phone wasn't that good, so it couldn't record for that long, but Seeker really liked how he looked when he was painting. The way the paint came out of the cans, he thought his hands looked like Spider-Man's.

Seeker knew he should finish up his work. It looked okay. Even before he finished he could tell that he hadn't made it look like he had on the napkin. It was too involved for him and he needed more time.

Still, as he stared at what he'd drawn on the wall, Seeker realized that he had come close.

"To a lot of people it would probably look like his name was springing up from the water." He thought.

Seeker was gonna continue working on this. He'd continue drawing it napkins and tagging it around town. Eventually he'd get it right.

Chapter 16.

"Javier wants a piece of you, Sergio." Gustavo Bustos said as Seeker walked by him.

Gustavo wasn't in a gang. Seeker didn't really know him that well, but they weren't not friends. Gustavo was bigger than most of the students at Cutter Middle School. He was an Eighth grader but he looked like he could be a junior in High School.

"So." Seeker said. He bent down to tie his shoe. "He's always after someone."

"You're the big dog now." Gustavo smiled.

"Yup." Seeker smiled and kept on walking.

"Javier says he's gonna get all you guys." Gustavo continued. "Then when Hector comes back he won't have the Little Killerz. He won't have nothing."

Seeker just continued walking. He tried to have the same calm walk that he always had. It wasn't working. He felt like everybody was looking at him.

Like he had a target on his back.

Chapter 17.

Angel and Seeker settled into their seats in the movie theater. They were watching "The Dark Knight Rises." Seeker had seen it a bunch of times but never with Angel.

It had been out forever. Seeker couldn't see it until it came to the $3 theater by his house. He and Angel had to buy tickets to see "Ice Age: Continental Drift." Then they snuck into "The Dark Knight Rises" because it was rated R. That made going to the movies even more fun.

They lights had barely gone down when Angel grabbed him. Before Seeker could even take a sip of his soda they were making out.

"Her mouth was so wet, so warm... she always tastes so good." He thought.

Angel moved her hand in places nobody in the theater could see.

Seeker pulled away. Not because he didn't want her doing it... he was just startled. She smiled at him and kept going.

Angel and Seeker had never talked about the other guys she'd been with. Even other boyfriends. Seeker was kind of curious but Angel never mentioned them. It was like she lived in the moment, and if you weren't with her than you didn't exist.

Seeker knew she had gone out with older guys. He had seen her around town with them. Back then he used to just watch her and wonder what it would be like to be that guy.

Now he was that guy... but it was different than he thought it would be. Seeker and Angel were both 13 but she was a lot older than he was.

She had a reputation. Angel was known for going farther than a lot of the girls her age. Seeker wondered if she knew she had it. He wondered if it bothered her.

As she kissed his neck, he laid back even more in the seat.

He loved the opening scene of "The Dark Knight Rises." The way Bane appeared. How he seemed to destroy an airplane all by himself. As it played on the screen, the noise from it washing over them, Angel didn't even look at it. It could have been anything up there. The movie theater was dark and that was all she needed,

Seeker and Angel began to French kiss again. She was almost on top of him now.

He started to think she might want to have sex in the theater. It made sense. Angel was way more free and adventurous about this stuff than Seeker was.

Seeker could paint on a wall anywhere, anytime. As long as the cops weren't too close he had no fear.

Something about Angel, having sex with her, scared him.

He was worried that if he didn't do it his friends would never let him live it down. Seeker felt that he probably would be with her... even though he didn't know how ready he was. He loved Angel. He thought he did anyway.

Seeker was more worried about what having sex with her might do to his life? What if he got her pregnant?

Then he'd be trapped.

Just like his sister and Mario.

Just like her husband.

Just like Angel's sisters who both had kids.

Just like his father probably was.

From the glow of the screen, Seeker could see the grin in Angel's eyes as she moved herself against him. She knew what she was doing. She knew how excited Seeker was. Angel knew that she did this to all the guys.

She slowly moved herself down Seeker's body.

Seeker stared at the movie screen. As he watched one of his favorite movies Seeker could hardly concentrate.

Angel was doing things to him he had never experienced with another person before.

Seeker was glad the movie theater was dark. He was also glad that he and Angel were sitting in the back of it.

Chapter 18.

For some reason Seeker was having one of those days when he just wasn't on it.

He'd gotten up late. He'd gotten to school late. He didn't done a bunch of his assignments. He didn't eat breakfast. He had to spend so much time talking to his History teacher that he missed snack. So on top of everything else he was hungry and lunch was over two hours a way.

All of this was because he'd been out late with Angel. He didn't get home until almost one in the morning. They didn't have sex.

"The Dark Knight Rises" got out after ten. Angel had wanted to go somewhere and do it but they couldn't find a place. People were at her house and his house.

She suggested going to the park. Seeker didn't really want to but he didn't want to disappoint Angel. As they approached it Seeker saw that a bunch of the Owen Street Hoods were hanging out there.

He and Angel turned around and continued walking. They walked for so long that she seemed to lose interest in being with him. Eventually, she started to text her friends and then they decided to just go home.

They had spent about five hours together. Seeker was stoked because they'd had a good talk. He felt like they were getting closer. Before that night he didn't know that the father Angel lived with was really her stepfather. Her real dad was in jail. Seeker also didn't know that she wanted to make clothes when she got older.

"It makes sense," He thought. "She looks great in everything she wears."

Seeker joked that they should get married. They could move to a big city. He'd have a ton of places he could paint and she could make clothes for a big company. She didn't seem like that idea bothered her at all. Angel wanted them to own two big dogs.

It was in math that Seeker got the idea to try and get some food from the cafeteria. Seeker told the teacher, Mr. Hermann, that he needed to use the bathroom. He figured if he was really quick, he could get his food in the time it took him to normally go.

The ladies who ran the cafeteria liked him. Seeker figured if they saw him they'd take pity and give him some food. He never paid for his lunch anyway. He swiped his ID card. Hector, Anthony, Irvin, Nathan… none of his friends paid for the food they got at Cutter. They were just taken care of.

Seeker went over to the cafeteria and was bummed to find that it was locked up. He knocked on the door. Nobody opened it.

As he turned to go back to math, Principal Fry walked up.

"What are you doing out of class?" Principal Fry didn't sound mad. He sounded like he wanted an answer.

"I don't know.”

Principal Fry smiled. He knew Seeker too well.

"You don't know?" Principal Fry laughed. "You just got up and walked out of class?"

"No, I got permission.”

"You got permission to walk over to the lunch area?"

"I missed snack." Seeker said.

"Did you tell your teacher that?"

"No."

"What'd you say?"

"I said I needed to use the bathroom."

"Sergio, you and I both know that you shouldn't be out of class right now." Principal Fry's tone was starting to be less friendly.

"Maybe he's in a bad mood?" Seeker wondered. "Maybe he'll take it out on me?"

"I was hungry. I didn't eat breakfast." Seeker thought Principal Fry might let this go.

"I missed breakfast, too." Principal Fry's tone was still stern. "I still showed up for work on time."

At that moment Mr. Setari walked passed them. Seeker was about to look away. Then he changed his mind.

"Hi, Mr. Setari." Seeker said.

"Hey Sergio." Mr. Setari smiled. He walked over to them.

"I've known him from a long time ago." Seeker told Principal Fry. He was hoping this might help him somehow.

"Really?" Principal Fry looked at Mr. Setari. He didn't seem like he believed Seeker.

"Yeah," Mr. Setari eyed Seeker. He knew something was up. "We met when you were in the Third grade, right?"

"Yeah." Seeker said.

"He's changed a little bit since then." Principal Fry's tone was softening.

"He's a great kid." Mr. Setari said. "He's a little too cool sometimes, but overall he's still the Sergio I remember."

Seeker smiled at Mr. Setari. He may not have wanted to be seen talking to him in public, but all the students knew you did what you had to do if Principal Fry had you on the hook.

"Alright," Principal Fry started. "If you're gonna vouch for him that's enough for me."

Seeker was off the hook now.

"Why don't you go back to class? I'll bring a snack over to you."

"Thanks." Seeker said.

As he walked away, he could barely contain his smile. Here he'd gone and done something stupid and it had actually helped him.

"Who cares if people see Principal Fry giving me something?" Seeker laughed to himself. "He runs the school. Nobody else is having him bring them a snack in class."

Chapter 19.

As he sat in Del Taco with Anthony, Irvin and Nathan, Seeker continued to work on his new tag. His name emerging from water.

They were waiting for Hector. This had become an afternoon routine. They would go to school and then meet Hector to tell him what they'd done that day.

"If he cared so much he probably shouldn't have gotten suspended." Seeker thought to himself. He knew he couldn't tell that to the other guys in the Little Killerz. "They'll tell Hector for sure."

"Maybe he's not coming?" Anthony said.

Seeker was surprised. He thought these guys would wait hours for Hector without asking any questions.

"He'll be here." Seeker didn't look up from what he was drawing.

Anthony, Irvin and Nathan had pooled their money to buy a small order of fries and a coke. They passed the cup back and forth. Seeker was just having water.

Seeker was really into his drawing. He'd probably gone through 10 napkins at that Del Taco alone. He felt he was really close to making it look just the way he wanted it to.

"I'm starving." Irvin stated. "I wish we had more than just fries."

"Didn't you eat lunch?" Nathan asked.

"Yeah, but I'm still hungry."

"Tell them you're hungry." Anthony said.

That comment got Seeker's attention.

"What's that gonna do?" He asked.

"Tommy Pike said that he was in Del Taco with his mom and his baby brother. His mom didn't have enough for a drink. The lady behind the counter felt bad and gave her one free."

"So you think if Irvin tells the people here that he's hungry, they'll just give him a free meal?" Seeker wondered if this was a law that restaurants couldn't turn down young people that needed food.

"He's kid." Anthony started. "A restaurant has to feed kids who are hungry."

"Who says?" Nathan asked.

"They have to." Anthony stated emphatically. "My dad told me."

"Is that how your family gets all your food?" Seeker smiled. Nathan and Irvin laughed.

"Shut up." Anthony said.

"I'm just playin'." Seeker offered.

Hector walked into the Del Taco. He came over to the table. Anthony, Irvin and Nathan scrambled to make room for him.

"How does this happen?" Seeker wondered. "How do you go from playing with somebody on the swings in elementary school to worshipping them when they get a little older?"

"What's up?" Hector asked. He ate some of the remaining fries.

"Not much." Seeker said. "What's up with you?"

"Nothing. I'm tired of being at home."

Hector seemed especially edgy today. Seeker figured his dad or his brothers had beat on him or something. Hector was tough but more than anything he had a big mouth. His family wouldn't put up with either of those things for a second. It was probably why Hector was always in so much trouble. He'd been beaten up so many times by his dad that he felt like he had something to prove. That he had to show other people who was the boss. Seeker had been over Hector's house enough to know that his dad wasn't the nicest person. It wouldn't take much for him to put Hector in his place.

"They still expect me to do my homework. They told my mom I'll get behind if I don't get it done." Hector went on.

"Are you doing it?" Nathan asked.

"A little. I wish I could drop out." Hector said. "Be a full time gangster."

Anthony, Irvin and Nathan, as if on cue, all chimed in with how cool that would be to not have to go to school anymore.

"Wouldn't you be even more bored then?" Seeker asked. He wasn't trying to point out how Hector had contradicted himself. He just said it.

"I'd get a job at least."

"You can get a job when you're 13?" Irvin asked.

"I'm 14, almost 15. Besides there's lots of jobs you can do when you're our age." Hector smiled after he said that.

He was referring to dealing drugs. A lot of dealers liked using young kids. Nobody really suspected them and if they got caught they were so young that nothing bad really happened.

"What about that teacher you want to get?" Anthony asked.

Seeker wanted to kick Anthony under the table for bringing that up.

"Yeah Seeker," Hector eyed him. "What's up with that?"

"I haven't found out what car he drives yet." Seeker knew it was a weak excuse. He didn't have the guts to tell Hector that he didn't want to find out either.

"How hard it is it to follow him after school and see what he drives?" Nathan asked.

"It isn't hard," Seeker started, mad that Nathan opened his big mouth. "If they leave after school. Mr. Setari doesn't. He stays in his room. And you know Mr. Robert. You can only hang around the school if you're in a group or if you're getting picked up. I gotta bail when the bell rings. Why don't you find out what car he drives, Nathan? If it's so easy."

Nobody Seeker knew got picked up by their parents. And none of them were in the homework club or played sports after school.

"It's not like I can just ask someone who does stay after school to do this." He offered.

There was silence at the table. Hector was clearly upset that Seeker hadn't done what he'd asked him to do. He knew Hector thought that whatever ground the Little Killerz had at Cutter was being lost to the Owen Street Hoods. Every day that Hector wasn't there was another day that he lost more of what he thought he had.

Chapter 20.

After eating at Del Taco the Little Killerz went to the supermarket. It was in the same strip mall as the Del Taco they always hung out in. They stole some candy and some sodas. Hector stole some cigarettes. Irvin wanted to steal some beer but none of them had anything to hide it in. They'd done that before. Stuffed the beers in their backpacks and bailed. Then they went to their old elementary school and got buzzed.

The first few times Seeker had stole things it had been fun. That was five years ago. Now it just seemed like they were trying to get into trouble. Like Hector wanted to see how close they could come to getting busted.

Despite stealing stuff since they were really young, none of the Little Killerz had ever gotten in any real trouble. Hector was around all these tough, hard people, when he wasn't with the Little Killerz. His dad had been to jail a bunch of times. His brothers too. It seemed like Hector felt like he had something to live up to. Seeker had heard them laugh at Hector when he tried to talk tough. He figured that that was what made Hector act the way he did.

After hanging around the strip mall and the park, Anthony, Irvin and Nathan bailed. Seeker was alone with Hector. It had been awhile since just the two of them had hung out. They used to do everything together. Once the Little Killerz started the other guys were always around.

As they moved down the street, traffic was starting to pick up as people were coming home from work. The sun was about halfway down. Seeker loved this time of day when everything looked orange. It was also the best time to tag something because everybody was so busy trying to get home, nobody paid any attention to somebody like Seeker spray painting on the wall.

Monica Reyes and Sammi McQuade walked by them on the street.

"You guys should hold hands." Monica teased. Sammi cracked up.

Seeker thought Monica was pretty. She had semi-long brown hair and wore a lot of make-up. She also dressed like a girl who was a lot older than 12. Tight pants and a tight shirt that showed a little bit of her stomach. Seeker couldn't remember when he'd started noticing how much older all the girls around him looked.

Sammi was white and had red hair. She mostly wore jeans and sweatshirts. She barely ever spoke. She just laughed a lot at things Monica said.

"Shut up." Hector said before Seeker could make a sassy comment back to her.

Seeker knew that Hector wanted a girlfriend. Girls just didn't seem to like him.

"He's too mean." Seeker told himself. "Don't you understand Monica wants you to say something funny back to her?"

When they hung out together, girls always seemed to talk more to Seeker.

"Yeah," Seeker started. "You only hate cause you want us."

Monica and Sammi laughed as they kept walking down the street.

Seeker thought Hector might be mad because he didn't back him up with a harsh comment. Hector stared straight ahead. He had other things on his mind. He took out the box of cigarettes he'd stolen. They were still unopened.

"So," Hector started. "How well do you know that teacher?"

"What teacher?" Seeker knew Hector knew who he was talking about. He just didn't want to talk about this. Seeker didn't know what Hector wanted to do but, whatever it was, he wanted Hector's idea to go away.

"Don't be a punk." Hector socked Seeker in the arm. "The one that got me kicked out of school."

"Oh, Mr. Setari. I don't really know him. I just knew him from a long time ago."

"He talked to you. When I got sent to the office." Hector was eyeing him now. Seeker felt like he was under interrogation. He didn't want to say the wrong thing... have Hector catch him in a lie.

"I don't know."

"You gotta find out his ride." Hector smiled.

"Why?"

Hector's smile vanished.

"Because I'm asking you to."

Seeker stared Hector directly in the eyes. He hadn't wanted to but he'd made Hector mad. He had to cool him off. Fast.

"You just want me to find out what car he's driving? That's it?"

"Yeah."

Seeker started think about why Hector would want to know this? What he might want to do?

"You gonna trash his car?"

"Nah, that's nothing."

"Maybe you should just let this go?" Seeker finally said.

He had to say something. Seeker couldn't stand this conversation any longer.

"What?" Hector's tone was getting angrier.

"Why do you want to do this? You're already..."

Before the words were out of Seeker's mouth, Hector took him and threw him up against a fence along the sidewalk.

Hector's face was about an inch from Seeker's.

"Since when did you start telling me what to do?" Hector asked. "You think because I'm gone you're in charge of the Little Killerz now?"

His breath stank. If Seeker hadn't been so scared it probably would've bothered him.

"No. I'm not telling you what to do. I just want to know what you're planning. You're not at school. We don't talk as much. You know I'm down, Hector. Way more down than the other guys."

Hector continued to glare at him. It was that moment in a stand-off like this where things could go either way.

Hector laughed slightly.

"I'm sorry, bro." He let go of Seeker and moved away from him. "I just... I gotta get him while I'm bounced. This way they won't suspect me. Nobody can say they saw me doing nothing. It's gonna be totally gangster, like for real."

Seeker thought if Hector was gone that made him the prime suspect if anything happened to Mr. Setari's car. He wanted to tell him to chill but he'd already pissed off Hector once. Seeker wasn't looking to get thrown up against the fence again.

"Okay." Seeker said.

"I know you're down, Seeker." They started walking again. "I knew you weren't gonna let that ghetto teacher diss your homey."

"Yeah." Seeker said.

It wasn't until Seeker and Hector went their separate ways that Seeker felt better. Like he could breathe again.

Chapter 21.

Later that night Seeker went to Angel's house. They went to the park around the corner.

It looked like it had been nice at one time but it wasn't anymore. There were three swings and two of them were broken. The plastic slide (which had been called the big toy when Seeker was younger) was all marked up with graffiti. It also smelled like pee. Seeker knew this firsthand because he and some of the Little Killerz had peed down the slide a few years ago. The park also had a sandbox. It had been light colored when the park had first been set up, but it was so brown and gross people now called it "quicksand."

Seeker sat on a bench. Angel was sitting in his lap, straddling him. She was wearing a tight pair of jeans and a loose white shirt that hung off her dark body.

They were making out. It seemed like they had been making out for a long time. Seeker wondered if Angel was gonna tell him they should have sex. There was nobody in the park. A few kids had ridden by on their bikes awhile ago. Other than that, Seeker hadn't seen anybody.

If Angel did want to have sex, Seeker was ready to go. She got him so excited. Angel knew this and she loved it.

Seeker wished he could talk to her. Really talk to her. He didn't want to be in the Little Killerz anymore. He didn't want to have to fight people. And he certainly didn't want to hurt Mr. Setari.

"Why can't I just go to school like everybody else?" He wanted to ask.

He thought Angel could relate because they had a lot in common. They were both popular, they both came from families that were poor, they both lived with a lot of members of their family....

"Lets go away together." He said in between making out with her. Angel continued to kiss him. She didn't open her eyes. She didn't acknowledge a word he had said.

"I'm being serious." He continued. He pulled away from Angel. "I want to get out of here."

"Where would you go?" She asked, finally opening her eyes. Seeker loved Angel's eyes.

"You mean where would we go?" He smiled. "It wouldn't be forever. You don't ever want to get away from here? Even just for a day?"

"I go away sometimes. With my sister. She takes me up to LA to go shopping. She says in year she'll start taking me to clubs. She even has a fake ID I can use."

Seeker stared at Angel. It didn't seem like she thought about anything other than having fun. He didn't know how a conversation with his girlfriend was supposed to be, but he felt like something was missing with Angel. He'd always felt that way.

"Maybe I could go with you sometime? To LA?" He asked.

"Maybe." She smiled slyly.

Seeker knew she would say that. That was how Angel was. She never let people know that she needed them.

"I really like you." She said.

Angel kissed him nice and slow. She smelled so good. Her breath was perfect. It was a like a blend between mints and fruit.

He felt himself getting even more excited.

"Is it gonna be now?" He wondered.

Seeker told himself he was ready. He told himself that if Angel wanted him, if she wanted to have sex with him... he was gonna do it.

It wouldn't be for Hector or any of the Little Killerz. It wouldn't be for Angel. It would be for the two of them; because he wanted to be with Angel in that way.

"I love her." Seeker kept telling himself that.

He didn't say it to Angel, though. It would make him look too vulnerable.

"Did you bring anything?" She smiled.

Angel pulled back a bit so they could look at one another again.

Seeker stared at her. He didn't know what she meant at first.

Angel extended her index finger. She ran her hand over it as if she was covering it with something.

Condoms. Rubbers. Jimmy Hats.

Seeker had never even thought about that. It had never crossed his mind.

"What about the pill?" He asked.

"I don't take it."

"Oh."

"It makes me break out."

Seeker looked at Angel's pristine complexion. Her face never had a blemish.

"Bring some next time... and I'll rock your world."

"Okay." Seeker said.

At that moment, with Angel straddling him in the park, whatever Angel wanted him to do he would've done.

Chapter 22.

Seeker had a tough time walking home after being with Angel.

He had never been that close to doing it.

Seeker had gotten himself so excited that he thought he might have hurt himself. He had a lot of pain between his "lower area" and his stomach. He felt like somebody had kicked him in the groin.

He had remembered hearing about this from some of the older guys that lived on his street.

They called it "blue balls."

Seeker had expected to feel it there. He didn't. It was above them and it hurt.

When he finally made it home he laid down. Seeker wanted to take something for it. The only reason that he didn't was because his sister in the living room and he was embarrassed.

"I can't tell her about this." He told himself. If he did he thought that she would laugh.

Seeker just lay in bed. He stared up at the ceiling in the darkness of his room. The only sounds he heard were his nephews playing video games in the living room.

He just wanted the pain to go away. Seeker wanted to be asleep before his nephews came in the room. He couldn't imagine how much it would suck to listen to them and be in pain like he was.

Seeker closed his eyes. He must've been really tired because before he knew it he went to sleep. Pain and all.

The pain was gone when he woke up.

As he lay in bed he thought about Angel. He knew that he was going to be with her. They were bound to be alone again soon and he couldn't put off the inevitable. Seeker figured that she would eventually say that it was okay that he didn't have condoms. Seeker and her would have sex and he would probably get her pregnant.

Then he'd be stuck. He'd have to quit school or something. Seeker would have to provide for his family. He would never leave his neighborhood. He'd probably stop doing graffiti because he would be so busy working.

Before he started to really let these thoughts hit him, Seeker got out of bed. His room was dark. He could hear his nephews breathing as they slept.

Seeker went out into the living room. There was nobody there. He figured his sister was probably sleeping. His dad was most likely over at a friend's house or he was sleeping; if he was home.

Seeker turned on the lights in the living room. It was dirty. There were dirty plates, dirty clothes, and dirty kids toys all over the place. He didn't care about that.

Since Mario, his sister's boyfriend, was usually not there he often slept on the couch when he came in. Otherwise, he slept in the room with Seeker's sister. Mario always had a backpack sitting by the couch so he could have some things on hand if he needed them. It was filled with some clothes and things he didn't want to carry around.

There were condoms in there. Seeker had seen him take some out one time before he left for a few days. Mario didn't think anybody was watching him when he did that.

Seeker went over to the backpack, unzipped it, and felt around for the condoms.

He heard a noise.

"It'd be just my luck to run into my dad right now." He thought.

Seeker couldn't remember the last time it was just him and his dad alone. He couldn't remember the last time they had really talked about anything. Seeker's sister just signed his name if he brought home anything from school that needed to be signed by a parent.

There were no other noises. Seeker found the condoms and put two in his pocket.

As he walked back to his room he wondered if his brother-in-law was going to miss them.

"Maybe he counts them?"

Seeker didn't care. He wasn't gonna end up like him or anybody else in his family.

Chapter 23.

Seeker got lucky in a different way that Thursday.

School was out. He had to stay late to finish up a writing assignment in Mrs. Duckett's class.

"Sergio," he heard Mr. Setari call as he passed his class.

Seeker hadn't planned to do what Hector wanted him to do. At least not that day, but now seemed like as good a time as any to get it out of the way. Seeker figured Hector was gonna mess up his car or something. Maybe pop the tires or break a few windows. Nothing too bad.

"He probably wants everybody to think it's gonna be really gangster... but it won't be." Seeker told himself. "Hector always talks big."

He turned and walked over to Mr. Setari. Seeker wasn't sure how he was going to find out what kind of car he drove. If he came right out and asked that would look suspicious.

"How's it going?" Mr. Setari asked. He always seemed overly excited to be talking to Seeker.

"Like I make him cool or something." Seeker thought.

It was weird to him that he could make an adult feel cool. Usually it was the other way around. Young people were always trying to show how grown up they were.

"Good." Seeker said. "This is your room?"

"Yeah," Mr. Setari said.

He turned so Seeker could walk inside.

"Come on in."

Mr. Setari walked into his room. Seeker looked around real quick to make sure nobody had seen him enter it. Mr. Setari's back was turned so he didn't see this.

"We're reading a book called 'The Outsiders.'" Mr. Setari said.

He pointed to a bunch of drawings of tough and rich looking kids. Some of the student's written assignments were also on the walls.

"I read that last year in seventh." Seeker continued to stare at the drawings. He was trying to see if they resembled the actors in the movie.

"Did you like it?"

"It was okay. I liked the movie better. I liked drawing the characters."

"I'll bet you were really good at that. You were drawing great stuff in that summer school class years ago." Mr. Setari smiled.

"It was cool."

"I remember you were really into that Bakugan game then, too. You still into that?"

"How old do you think I am?" Seeker wanted to ask.

He started to think it was a mistake coming into Mr. Setari's class. Seeker didn't want to get Hector that information. Even worse than that was being treated like he was still a little kid.

"If only he knew that he's treating me that way?" Seeker wondered. "Maybe we could be friends now? Maybe Mr. Setari wouldn't be so stuck in the past?"

"Nah." Seeker said to Mr. Setari.

Mr. Setari's cell phone rang. It was in his hand. He looked at it.

"I better get going. That's my wife."

Mr. Setari put his phone in his pocket.

"Okay." Seeker said.

Mr. Setari grabbed his bag and they walked out of his class. He turned off the lights and shut the door.

Seeker hadn't wanted to walk through the school with Mr. Setari, but he had to if he was going to find out what car he drove.

As they walked Seeker saw that there weren't that many students around.

"Just nerds in the homework club after school." He told himself.

"You excited about the dance coming up?"

"I guess."

Seeker hadn't ever really thought about them. He didn't go to too many school dances. They were too expensive. Aside from Angel... the only thing that really got him excited was graffiti. A lot of people he knew wouldn't understand that. It was part of why Seeker didn't really share his drawings or graffiti art with people. They knew he did it but they didn't understand that he had to do it.

"Wait until you get to high school. Everything's different there." Mr. Setari said. "The dances are bigger. You have more freedom around campus; more classes, more electives. You can take an art class. You'll ace that."

"That'd be cool."

They approached the parking lot in front of the school. There were only a few cars there.

"This'll make finding his car easier." Seeker told himself.

"I got something for you." Mr. Setari reached into his bag. He pulled out a small, black sketchbook. He handed it to Seeker. "I want you to fill it up with your drawings."

"Okay. Thank you." Seeker said.

He was really stoked. Seeker was always drawing on napkins and scraps of paper. Now he had a cool book to do it in. It was small enough for him to take anywhere.

Mr. Setari held up his hand and Seeker high fived him.

"See you tomorrow." Mr. Setari said.

He turned and walked toward his car.

Seeker turned and made it look like he was walking away. He lingered behind a brick wall that was attached to a school gate.

He watched Mr. Setari walk over to his car. It was a white Kia. Mr. Setari tossed his bag into the front seat and got inside.

Chapter 24.

The talk with Mr. Setari had stressed Seeker out. On his walk home from school he decided that he needed to do something to relax.

So he went to Home Depot.

Seeker wasn't a thief but he'd used up all his spray paint on his last tag. With the exception of a few things from liquor stores and supermarkets by his house, he'd never really stolen anything.

Except spray paint.

If he could work he would pay for it. He wasn't old enough.

If there was a way to do chores and get the money he would do that. There was nobody at his house that was gonna pay him to do that.

The trick to stealing spray paint was not to take too much at once. Thankfully, Seeker didn't need much, just a few cans of black.

He was still working on making his name look like it was coming out of the water. Seeker needed the blue paint so it looked like there was water around it. He needed the black paint so that it gave his name depth.

Seeker quickly walked through the store and found the paint he needed. He hadn't been in this Home Depot in awhile. Thankfully, there were other stores he could steal paint from. He tried to make it as random as possible.

Then, rather than take the paint somewhere to take the security tags off, he walked around the store doing it. Seeker didn't look at the cans as he did it. This way he wouldn't look suspicious. Sometimes it took awhile for the tags to come off but Seeker could wait.

Seeker always kept his nails kind of long. He would slide them under the security tag and then discreetly peel them off.

Seeker then dropped them around some other part of the store. Sometimes the end of the tag went too far in and it jabbed into his skin. That hurt. It was better than trying to take the tags off with a knife or something. If he got caught with that on him, even if he wasn't doing anything, he'd be in a lot more trouble.

Once the tags were gone he went to the most secluded area of whatever store he was in, made sure there were no cameras around, and put the spray paint cans inside his bag. He never went in the bathroom. That was too suspicious. Plus, the bathrooms had sensors in front of them for the tags and he didn't want to chance setting one off. If Seeker did that he knew getting out of the store would be impossible.

Once he put the spray paint cans in his backpack he didn't leave the store right away. He'd walk around. Seeker might even ask a clerk some questions about a product or something. He'd say he was doing a project for school. People were usually eager to help. Some of them knew him a little bit. Seeker figured that might help him if he ever got caught.

Sometimes, if he happened to have some money on him, he might buy something like a box or a lightbulb.

Eventually, when Seeker felt like he'd been in the store long enough he'd hold his breath and walk out.

The alarm had never gone off on him.

And it didn't today.

It was time to paint.

Seeker had earned that.

Chapter 25.

Seeker was eating lunch with Angel and the other members of the Little Killerz. A lot of times they walked around as they ate. They'd go out into the field, or maybe on to the blacktop. They had to sneak their food out there.

Today they were hanging out around a planter.

"Did you find out that stuff for Hector?" Anthony asked. "About that teacher?"

Seeker nodded his head. He didn't want to talk about it. He'd told Hector what car Mr. Setari drove. Seeker was hoping it would go away. That maybe Hector would get his mind on something else.

"It's never good to do something bad and have everybody know about it." He wanted to say. "Even though he's bounced the heat's on Hector. He should just stay down and let this go."

This is why he thought being in the Little Killerz was kind of lame. Anthony, Irvin and Nathan were followers. They just wanted to belong to something.

Seeker didn't care about that. He just wanted to paint and have everything be okay in his life. The Little Killerz just seemed to complicate that. He wanted to quit but then he'd not only have no friends… he'd have enemies.

"I'm already in," He told himself. "No point in crying now."

"What does Hector want to do?" Angel asked.

"I don't know." Seeker was trying to think of anything he possibly could to change the subject.

"You guys wanna see the new 'Star Wars'?" He asked.

Everybody stared at him, confused that he'd changed the subject so abruptly.

"Is it out?" Nathan asked.

"It will be… in 2015." Seeker said.

None of the Little Killerz watched movies like he did. Angel liked movies but she didn't really think about them.

"Those movies are boring." Anthony said.

"No they're not!" Seeker said. He said it so loud he thought he sounded like Hector. "They're the best movies ever."

"No way!" Irvin said. "That was 'The Avengers.'"

"The Avengers?" Seeker couldn't believe Anthony said that. "None of those guys are as cool as Luke Skywalker, Anakin, Han Solo, or Darth Vader!!"

"Seeker!" A voice called.

He looked behind him. Javier was standing there. A few of the Owen Street Hoods were behind him.

Chapter 26.

Seeker faced Javier as the Little Killers stood behind him.

"We shouldn't fight here." Seeker started. "You know the rules."

Javier smiled.

"What makes you think I want to fight?"

"You're with your boys; calling me out."

"You're with yours." Javier pointed to the members of the Little Killerz.

"What's up?" Seeker asked.

"Hector's gone."

"He'll be back; soon." Seeker hated having to talk like this. Speaking for Hector; pretending to be tough.

"Who cares about any of this?" He wanted to say. "Lets just be friends and hang out like a couple of years ago?"

"Yeah... and we'll still be here. There's strength in numbers." Javier looked at all the members of the Little Killerz as he spoke. "You guys should join up. Hector too. We'll all be Owen Street. You guys can be real gangsters."

"Yeah," Seeker thought to himself. "Like Hector's gonna ever follow you."

He didn't say that. Seeker had to represent the Little Killerz. He had to have Hector's back.

Seeker had to be down.

"That sounds great." Seeker said.

He could almost hear the other Little Killerz asking themselves, "It does?"

"Cool." Javier said.

"There's just one problem." Seeker smiled slightly. "We're not from Owen Street. And we don't want to be."

Javier stared at Seeker hard. Seeker had dissed him in front of everybody.

Seeker turned his body slightly. If Javier pushed him or started going off, Seeker wanted to be ready.

"Principal Fry." One of the Hoodz said to Javier.

Javier looked past Seeker now. Seeker didn't take his eyes off of him.

At that moment Seeker could've made quite a name for himself if we would've decked Javier. He'd have beaten up the leader of a rival gang AND done it in front of Principal Fry. This would've served notice to anybody who messed with him that Seeker didn't care. That he was just as tough as Hector who'd also beat up Javier.

Seeker did care, though. Javier wasn't worth it.

"Well," Javier shrugged. "You guys had your chance."

He turned and the rest of the Owen Street Hoodz walked away from them.

"Damn," Anthony said. He shook Seeker's hand. "That was gangster the way you handled those guys."

Angel put her arms around his waist. Seeker wrapped his arm around her shoulder. He was the leader.

The bell rang.

Everybody took off for their classes.

Seeker and Angel, still entwined, walked together even though they didn't share a class.

"You get those things?" Angel asked.

Seeker looked at her and smiled. He nodded his head.

"Meet me at the gate after school."

"Why?" Seeker knew why but he wanted to hear her say it.

"So I can rock your world."

She kissed him softly on the lips and then broke away.

Seeker watched as she walked over to her class. Angel turned back to him and laughed a little.

"One minute!" Seeker heard Mr. Robert yell across the campus.

Seeker barely made it in time.

Chapter 27.

Seeker could barely concentrate in Biology.

"Am I really gonna do it?" He asked himself. "Do I want to do it?"

Seeker did want to do it. He just wanted it to be more than what Angel was making it.

"What's the point of having sex if it's gonna possibly get us in trouble?"

He wasn't worried about their parents. Seeker knew that her mom would probably be happy if she got pregnant and his dad wouldn't care. It wasn't like he was going to help out anyway. Seeker's dad hadn't been any help with his sister's kids.

"It's going to be great being with Angel..." He told himself.

Seeker looked around the classroom and wondered how far some of his classmates had gone.

"Some of them had to have had sex before."

He knew that after having sex for the first time, no matter what, things would never be the same again.

Sergio "Seeker" Torres would never be same again.

He was scared that by sharing himself with Angel like that, he was going to be giving up a part of himself forever. And no matter how hard he tried he'd never get that back.

Chapter 28.

Seeker was on top of Angel. Her shirt was off. Her skin was so soft against his. She was wearing a bra and a short skirt. This wasn't the first time Seeker had seen almost seen all of Angel's body. Even though she dressed in a way that didn't leave a lot to the imagination, he was still in awe of how incredible she was.

"She's probably going to be even more beautiful when she gets older." He thought to himself. "If that's possible."

That thought alone was enough to get him excited.

They were making out on the floor of Angel's bedroom. She shared it with her older sister, Maribel. Seeker wondered when she was going to be home.

He wished they could be in her bed. Angel hadn't prepared for this. Her and Maribel's clothes were everywhere; on the bed, on the floor, under the bed, etc. The minute they went into her room Angel had basically pulled him to the ground.

Even as he worried that her sister might come home, that even using a condom he might impregnate her, that he might be trapped into the very life he hoped to escape, Seeker was ready to go.

However, this wasn't how he thought his first time was going to be. Seeker didn't know what to expect, but he had a feeling it was going to be over a lot quicker than he wanted it to be.

"And then... after that... will I still be special to Angel?" Seeker wondered a lot about that.

"I want you so bad, Seeker..." Angel whispered in his ear.

"I love you, Angel." Seeker meant it. He wanted to be more than close with Angel. He wanted to be connected to her. To know, despite his doubts, that she really cared about him.

Maybe sex was the way?

"I love you, too." She said in-between their slow kisses.

He unzipped his pants to put his condom on.

Seeker started getting even more excited.

"I'm really going to do it." He told himself. "Angel and I are going to make love on the floor of her bedroom. It's not perfect... but she is."

Then his cell phone rang. He had a text. Seeker hadn't put it on vibrate. It was playing some dumb ringer. It was totally killing the mood that was set by the Frank Ocean CD Angel put on.

"Turn that off!" Angel was annoyed. Seeker didn't like when she talked to him like that.

As he turned off the ringer, Seeker saw that he had a text.

It was from Hector. He wanted to have meeting with the Little Killerz.

Now.

Chapter 29.

"Seeker!!" Angel said angrily as he sat up in front of her. She was laid out in front of him. Half naked. Ready to go.

"Look, Hector wants to meet and I don't want to rush through this!" Seeker hoped that if he sounded mad enough that would put Angel in check.

"Well..." He could see she was trying not to show how angry she was. "Are you gonna come back?"

"Yeah." He smiled. "Will your family be here?"

"Not if you're back in soon." Angel curled up a bit on the floor. "Just hurry back, Seeker. I wanna do this."

"Me too."

Before he knew it, Seeker was on the street again running to meet with the Little Killerz.

The pipe bomb Hector was holding looked ghetto.

Seeker should've known that Hector had something he didn't want a lot of people to see. That was why he had called a meeting at the river trail. Except for some bums and winos that came through there, it was almost always empty.

The pipe bomb was less then a foot long. The caps on the top and bottom had what looked like wet glue around them. At the top was a fuse that looked like it might be too long. Hector seemed like he was holding it in a certain way so that it would stay attached.

As Seeker stared at it he tried to figure out what Hector might want it for. Hector had shown them guns he had gotten before; brass knuckles, butterfly knives... but they were for show. As far as he knew, Hector was fencing them for somebody.

"Why would he have a pipe bomb?" Seeker kept asking himself.

When he'd shown up Hector was already showing it around.

"That thing's gangster." Irvin said.

"How'd you make that?" Nathan asked.

"I looked it up on the internet." Hector laughed. "I felt like a terrorist."

He smiled after he said that.

"Why do you have it?" Seeker asked. He knew that none of the other guys would have the guts.

"You know why." Hector seemed mad at Seeker. He was upset that he was late for the meeting.

"If only you guys knew what I was doing." Seeker wanted to say.

"Why?" Seeker pressed.

"For that teacher." Hector smiled after he said it. "Now that's being a real gangster."

All the Little Killerz seemed to look at Seeker at the same time. It was like everybody else knew what the pipe bomb was for.

Except for him.

"You can't do that." Seeker's tone was even.

Seeker and Hector stared at one another.

"Why not?" Hector twirled the bomb a bit in his hand.

"You're gonna kill Mr. Setari?" Seeker half-laughed. He hoped that that would be enough to diffuse the situation. Seeker didn't want to fight with Hector.

"No, I'm gonna blast that fool's ride."

"What if he's in it?"

"So what?"

"Hector," Seeker said the words before he realized what he was saying. "That's stupid."

Chapter 30.

"What'd you call me?!?!" Hector yelled.

He gripped the pipe bomb now and pushed Seeker back.

Then Hector pushed Seeker again.

He wanted the other members of the Little Killerz to stop Hector. To get between them and tell him that they were a gang; a team. They couldn't fight each other.

"I didn't call you stupid. I called what you wanted to do stupid and that's because it is, Hector."

Seeker glared back at him now. He hoped some of the Little Killerz might get between them before this got out of hand.

"You're a punk, Seeker. Picking that teacher over me." Hector handed the pipe bomb to Irvin.

Before Seeker knew what was happening, Hector slammed him in the face with his fist. It was quick and jarring.

Then Hector hit him again.

Hector was really quick. Seeker knew he was going to have to do something to slow him down.

Without thinking he grabbed Hector and head-butted him.

"Hey! Come on you guys!" Anthony said.

"Yeah, now you say something!" Seeker thought. "Where were you when he was hitting me in the face?"

Seeker felt blood from his nose roll down his lip. Hector had a large welt on his forehead. Seeker's head hurt a lot but at least he had slowed Hector down.

They stood across from one another with their hands in the air.

"Come on guys!" Irvin said.

Hector moved toward Seeker.

Seeker grabbed his arms so he couldn't throw any punches. Hector kicked Seeker. A lot.

Seeker was physically a lot bigger than Hector. This made it easier for him to move Hector around and contain him.

Seeker pushed Hector away from him so they could have more distance between them.

Nathan and Irvin got in front of him. Anthony ran over to Hector. Nathan and Irvin put their hands on Seeker to stop him. Anthony didn't lay a hand on Hector.

"You can't do this, Hector! It's stupid. I'm trying to help you!" Seeker wiped some blood from his nose.

"You're a punk, Seeker!! Go hang out with that punk teacher!! You're out of the Little Killerz!!" Hector screamed.

This is what Seeker wanted.

He was free.

But not really.

He stood there staring at Hector. His best friend since forever; his partner in crime. The person he was always down for.

Eventually, Seeker left the river trail.

He was out of the Little Killerz but he had feeling that wouldn't be the last time he had to deal with them.

Chapter 31.

Seeker went home, grabbed his backpack full of spray paint, and was out the door before anybody knew he was there.

He found an empty wall and in minutes he'd already drawn the skeleton of his name.

SeekeR.

His goal was still to make it look like it was coming out of water.

"This is all I have," he told himself. "It's the only thing that can take my mind off things."

As he painted it was almost a dance. He would think of a line he wanted to spray, a color he wanted to use, and in seconds that would appear in front of him. It was like Seeker's brain and his hands were completely in sync.

Then Seeker had a thought that almost disrupted everything. Angel.

"I told her I would come back." He remembered.

Seeker continued painting. He couldn't think about that now.

What he couldn't get out of his mind was how Angel wasn't somebody he thought he could count on.

"She's my girlfriend... shouldn't I be able to tell her my problems?" He asked himself.

Seeker knew that she wouldn't be any help. She liked who she thought Seeker was; the right hand man of Hector.

"Why can't my life be normal?!?" he wanted to scream.

Why couldn't anything in his life be normal?

His friendship with Hector.

His family.

School.

Angel.

"Why is everything so much easier in the movies?"

Seeker's thoughts fueled him as he continued to paint furiously. He imagined if anybody saw him they would think he was on drugs. He was moving so fast. He got such a rush from painting that he didn't care what anybody thought. Like he was so into it he couldn't be nervous. He didn't have time for that.

"Why can't Hector let things go?"

That was really the biggest thing on his mind. If he wasn't having problems with him he'd be fine. Seeker didn't want to be in the Little Killerz but at least when he was everything was fine.

Seeker was down but not in a good way now.

"Why did Mr. Setari have to come to Cutter this year?"

That thought made Seeker the angriest of all. If he had waited just one year, Seeker would've been out of there. He'd be at Murphy High School and everything would be fine. They never would've seen each other. Mr. Setari never would've pissed off Hector, and now Hector wouldn't want to blow up his car.

"Hector wants to blow up his car just cause he dissed him?!?" Seeker couldn't stop thinking about how lame all this stuff was. "This lame stuff is ruining my life."

Seeker's mind then switched to his family. That lifestyle. His sister, her husband, his dad... they were gonna stay in that apartment forever. They were never gonna leave it. Seeker had to get out of there but he didn't want to run away.

He had to keep painting. That was the key and he knew it. Seeker just had to focus and believe in himself.

Eventually, he finished that day's painting. His name looked a little more like it was emerging from the water but not 100%. It looked good but not great.

If Seeker was ever gonna do anything with his gift, deep down he knew that he was gonna have to be great.

Or at least try to be.

Chapter 32.

Seeker was slowly walking home as the sun went down.

Actually, he felt more like he was drifting.

Painting usually made him feel better.

He felt good; like he had released some of the angst and anger that had come over him that afternoon.

Seeker didn't feel great and that was the biggest difference; just feeling okay.

His phone rang. At first Seeker didn't want to answer it but he knew he had to.

"What happened to you?" Angel asked angrily. "You said you would come back?"

"You sound like we're married." He wanted to say.

He didn't.

"Hector needed to talk to me."

"For three hours?" Angel was getting madder. Seeker wanted to get off the phone. Fast.

"Listen can I call you back?" He wanted to be more forceful like how Mario sometimes was with his sister. The minute she questioned him about anything... where he was? Who he was with? Mario shot her down. Told her it was none of her business.

Seeker couldn't be that way.

"What's the matter?" Angel asked.

This surprised Seeker and it actually made him madder.

"Look Angel... it's really complicated."

"So tell me about it? Is something up with Hector? Or the Little Killerz?"

"Angel…." He just wanted to hang up the phone.

"Lets meet at the park? There's too many people at my house. You can tell me about it there." There was something in

Angel's voice. Something that Seeker hoped was actually genuine.

"Okay." He said. "I'll meet you at the park."

Chapter 33.

It didn't take Seeker long to realize that Angel didn't want to meet him at the park to talk.

She was on top of him as they were on a blanket that she'd brought from home.

There was nobody at the park. The more they kissed the more Seeker realized that she was expecting that they were going to resume where they left off. He'd have no excuse now.

Hector wasn't going to text him again. His family never worried about where he was. Nobody was going to help him.

Angel's kisses were getting more and more passionate.

When he met her there he was really hoping they would talk; at least a little.

It never happened. She had already put out the blanket and was waiting for him. No guy had probably ever turned Angel down and she wasn't going to let Seeker be the first.

Then, as if he couldn't help himself, Seeker pulled away from her.

"What's the matter?" She asked angrily.

"I thought we were gonna talk? I thought you wanted to know what happened to me today?"

"You'd rather talk than be with me?"

Angel couldn't imagine why Seeker was acting like this.

"You have anything with you?" She smiled. Seeker knew what she was talking about.

The rubbers.

"No," Seeker lied.

He just didn't want to do it today.

"Any other day but today." He thought to himself. "Too much has already gone wrong."

"That's okay," Angel smiled. "I stole some from my brother."

Angel reached into her pocket and pulled out a few condoms that were attached to one another.

She started moving down on Seeker again. Just like in the movie theater.

"Hey..." Seeker said. His voice was so low she didn't hear him.

He heard her pull open the condom packaging.

"Angel!" Seeker said louder.

Again she didn't respond.

Seeker realized that she wasn't going to. She was going to get what she wanted.

He sat up.

"Angel, stop!" He said.

Seeker's body moved so that Angel was on his legs now.

"What are you doing?" She was angry at him all over again.

Everybody was angry at Seeker today.

"I'm just not into it right now."

"Why not?"

"Because I'm not. Why can't we ever just hang out and talk? I don't even really know you, Angel."

"You'll get to know me." She smiled as she moved up on him. "Really well if you'd stop being such a baby."

"I just want this to be different. I don't want to be just another guy to you. If we're gonna do it I want it to matter."

"You don't think it's gonna matter to me?" She seemed hurt.

"I don't know, Angel. I don't know you. I do know that I don't want to be trapped, and if I get you pregnant that's exactly what I'll be. We'll both be trapped."

"You think I'm trying to trap you, Seeker?" Angel was furious now.

She stood up.

"I can do way better than you. I was just being nice but I can see that you don't want that."

"Angel, I do." He stood up. "You're taking this wrong. I want to be with you just not like this."

"Not like what? In a park? I'll bet Hector wouldn't mind. I'll bet none of the Little Killerz would mind; except you. You think you're so much better than everybody. Nobody's good enough for you. The truth is you probably don't even like girls."

Seeker stared at her. He thought about arguing but nothing he was gonna say would change Angel's mind about how she felt about him now.

"Forget it." He said. "I can't talk to you anyway."

Seeker turned and walked out of the park.

"Walk away, Seeker." She yelled at him. "I'm gonna tell everybody. You had a chance and you couldn't handle it. You're not a man. You're just a little, ghetto punk."

She yelled at Seeker all the way out of the park.

"I'm not a man," he told himself. "I'm too young to deal with all this stuff."

Chapter 34.

"Sergio," Mr. Robert said with a smile. "You get something to eat yet?"

Most of the time Mr. Robert was all business. He was nice to Seeker and his friends but he wasn't too nice.

"Not yet." Seeker said. "I had to do some work in English."

"You better hurry." Mr. Robert was back to being all business. Seeker knew that he meant it. If Seeker ended up being late to class he knew that Mr. Robert would be there to make him pay for it.

Detention was the last thing he needed. These days, being on the outs with the Little Killerz and Angel, Seeker didn't want to be at school any longer than he had to be. So far he hadn't run into any of them that morning.

Seeker didn't tell Mr. Robert that he wasn't going to be having a snack. He wanted to talk to Mr. Setari.

Seeker's heart sank the minute he walked into his classroom. Mr. Setari and Miss Weaver were standing across his desk talking.

He wasn't gonna get to talk to Mr. Setari. Seeker wouldn't be able to help him like he'd hoped.

"Hey Sergio," Mr. Setari said looking over at him.

"Hey." Seeker said.

"You need something?"

"I was just coming by to say 'Hi.' I'll see you later."

Seeker ducked out of the classroom.

"I guess I'll get snack after all." He told himself.

"Sergio..." Mr. Setari called.

Seeker turned around and looked at him. Mr. Setari was sticking his head out of his classroom.

"Everything okay?"

"He probably thinks he can help me again. Like he did when I was in 3rd grade." Seeker told himself. "He could help me. He could help himself; if he quit."

"Yeah." Seeker said.

Seeker turned and continued walking toward the snack area.

He had no idea that Anthony and Nathan had seen him talking with Mr. Setari. Had he known he would've also realized that they couldn't wait to tell Hector.

Chapter 35.

Seeker was lost in thought on his way home. He had fried his brain thinking about everything with Hector, Angel, Mr. Setari, his family, the Little Killerz.

He was all thought out.

Seeker started thinking about his drawings. The way his name looked on the wall. He had painted his name looking like it was emerging from the water in a few more places. It was looking a lot better than the first time he drew it.

"Still," He thought. "It could be better."

There was something about the way the water looked at is came off of it.

"It just doesn't look right." He kept telling himself.

If Seeker had to redo an assignment for school he hated doing it. Rewriting an English composition or something like that was awful.

With graffiti? Seeker loved it. He loved the feeling he got as he was doing it. So it didn't matter that he hadn't gotten his new design perfect. Maybe he never would? He just loved trying.

Seeker also knew the more he worked at it the better he got. Ever since he'd started people were impressed by what he did. They were always saying things like "That's gangster" or "How long did it take you to do that?"

Thinking about all of his graffiti work, Seeker had almost forgot about all his problems. Then some young girls, one with brown hair the same color as Angel's, ran past him.

Seeker hadn't really talked with anybody that day. If Angel was talking about him, saying he was scared to have sex with her or whatever, somebody would've come up to him and said something. That's just how middle school was. Once somebody said something, if it was juicy enough, all the students would be talking about it eventually.

"She'll look bad if she says something about me." Seeker reasoned. "I rejected her."

Even as he thought it, he couldn't believe he had turned Angel away. Seeker couldn't think of a single boy his age who would've done that. Sure, some people would probably say it was something he should be proud of, abstaining from sex, but that's not why Seeker didn't do it with Angel.

On a different day, if his head hadn't been so messed up, he probably would've been with her.

"I know I would. I was gonna have sex with her until Hector made me go to that stupid meeting."

Seeker told himself to stop thinking about this stuff. It wasn't going to do him any good. It was just bringing up his problems all over again.

As he started to think of something else, anything else, he saw Anthony in the distance.

The park where Seeker had been with Angel the night before was to his left. It was a small park with tiny sloping hills that were to the left of Seeker. He'd forgotten that Anthony lived close to it.

"Maybe I can talk to him?" Seeker thought. "Make things cool with Hector."

Then, out of the corner of Seeker's eye, he saw Irvin walking along one of the hills. He wore a different expression as he glared at Seeker. It let him know that something was coming.

"What's up, Seeker?" Hector called.

Seeker turned around and saw Hector and Nathan walking a few feet behind him.

"How'd they get there?" He wondered. Seeker hadn't seen them appear at all.

"Hey." Seeker said.

All of them were slowly moving toward him.

"Looks like you're getting jumped out, punk." Hector smiled.

They may have all been moving toward him but Hector got there first.

Chapter 36.

Hector slugged Seeker. Anthony kicked him. Irvin hit Seeker on the side of the head. Nathan hit whatever he could.

To anybody watching it would've looked like Seeker got his butt kicked. That the Little Killerz overwhelmed him. Seeker wanted to fight back but it was four against one. Him not throwing punches only seemed to make Hector more angry.

"Come on! Do something punk!" Hector yelled.

Seeker knew that no matter what he did he was gonna get a beating. All he had to do was take it.

Somehow, Seeker was still standing. Every so often he would make eye contact with Hector or one of the other guys.

That didn't help his cause. The punches and kicks kept coming.

Eventually, Seeker stumbled and fell to the ground. He covered up as the beating continued.

"That's for opening your mouth to that teacher!" Hector yelled as he and the others rained down punches. "Hope you like getting your ass beat for him!!"

The punches and kicks continued for a long time. Seeker was able to block a lot of them but the guys had done their damage.

Eventually, Seeker just felt one of them punching and kicking him.

"I think we got him Hector." Anthony said.

There was a long pause. Seeker half expected Hector to start hitting Anthony now.

"You got no one now, Sergio." Hector said. He knew that Seeker didn't like when people called him that. "No gang. No girl. Nothing. Later punk."

Then Hector spit on him.

Seeker heard their footsteps as all the Little Killerz walked away.

He wanted to get up but he was in too much pain. Seeker also wasn't in a hurry to go anywhere.

Seeker was on his own now. He had helped Mr. Setari... but he wasn't free.

Chapter 37.

Eventually Seeker stood up. The sun was going down. He squinted a bit as its rays hit his bruised and bloodied face. Seeker tried to steady himself.

He knew that if he went up the hill he would be going into the park. Seeker was turned around after the beating he'd got. If he kept walking into the park that would take him away from his house.

"I imagine that this is how Iron Man felt when he got beat up by Ivan Vanko in the second movie." He thought.

Seeker slowly turned his body and began walking home. Everything hurt.

Moving his legs. The way his feet hit the ground. The way Seeker held his shoulders. His face. His arms. His back. Even the wind as it blew a gentle breeze on him.

"It feels like every part of me is in pain."

Seeker kept moving little by little. He wanted to lie down again.

"Keep moving," He told himself. "Every little bit gets you home."

It was night by the time Seeker got to the apartment. It was also the longest walk home of his life.

He was thankful that his sister was in the kitchen and his nephews were lost in their video games. Aside from his sister saying "Hi," nobody seemed to even know that he had come into the house at all.

Seeker made it to his bedroom. He dropped face-down on his bed.

He wasn't bleeding that much anymore but he knew he was going to get his pillow and his sheets dirty.

For a moment he wondered what he was going to look like in the mirror. Then Seeker realized he didn't care.

The way he felt, the last person Seeker wanted to look at was himself.

Chapter 38.

Seeker didn't go to school for a couple of days after he got jumped out of the Little Killerz.

The first day he just stayed in bed while his sister took care of him. Seeker figured he must've looked pretty awful because his nephews stopped playing video games for the whole day and tended to him.

"So they got you? Did they have guns and stuff?" They asked.

"No. They just used their fists." Seeker didn't want to talk about it but his nephews were too young to see that.

"Let him rest." His sister finally yelled and whisked them out of the room.

She wanted him to tell her who beat him up. Seeker refused. She even threatened to cut off his cell phone. He still didn't tell her.

"Nobody's calling me anyway." Seeker told himself.

Seeker's Dad seemed startled for a moment when he first saw his son's face. Then he made a face of his own, shrugged like he didn't know what to say, and continued to watch the news on TV.

"He's probably bummed that his wimp son got beat up." Seeker thought.

Seeker wanted to tell his dad what was going on. He wanted to tell him about Hector, about Mr. Setari, about Angel...

He'd never told his dad anything. He never seemed to care. Seeker had tried a little bit when he was younger; if he got in trouble for something or if something made him sad. Seeker's dad never wanted to hear it.

Seeker had been really bummed since those guys beat him up. The things Angel said to him had also really hurt.

"She thinks I don't want to be with her because I don't like girls. Those guys beat me up and I didn't even fight back. Why can't I be more of a man? Then I'll have less problems."

These were thoughts that Seeker kept inside. Like he always did.

Before this, if he had a problem, he thought about it until he didn't want to think about it anymore or the problem went away.

"How did everything change so quickly?" He wondered.

These problems... they weren't going to change by themselves. Unless he did something to change them, they weren't going anywhere and Seeker knew it.

And that's what bothered him most of all.

Seeker had no idea what to do.

Chapter 39.

When he returned to school some people asked Seeker what happened to his face.

"What do you think?" Seeker asked.

He didn't want to talk about it. He also knew that the less he talked the less people would know that it was the Little Killerz that did it to him. They would find out eventually but he didn't want to be the one that told them.

The last thing Hector or any of those guys needed was to hear that Seeker had been talking smack. They'd probably beat him up again. They were probably already planning to.

"I'll be ready next time." He told himself. "I'll fight back at least. Those guys got a free shot and that was all they could do. If they try anything again... everybody'll see I'm no punk."

Seeker was so wrapped up in these thoughts as he ate his lunch alone at a planter, he didn't notice Javier and a bunch of the Owen Street Hoods surrounding him.

Chapter 40.

"Keep eating. Act like nothing's happening." Seeker told himself as he picked at his chicken nuggets and potatoes.

"What's up?" Javier eyed him.

"Hey." Seeker popped a nugget in his mouth. He took a drink from his chocolate milk.

"Where are your boys?" Javier smiled. He knew the answer. He just wanted to make Seeker squirm.

"If you want to fight you'll have to get in line." Seeker continued eating. "I'm not with those guys any more."

"Fight?" Javier continued with his fake smile. "You always think we want to fight you."

"Everybody else does." Seeker replied.

Seeker knew he sounded a lot tougher than he was. He knew that he had to do this. If he got a rep as somebody people could push around he'd be fighting all the time.

"I wanted to be on my own." Seeker told himself. "This is being on my own."

"I was thinking if you're not with the Little Killerz any more, you can join up with our set now." Javier stared at Seeker to gauge how he was taking this.

Seeker just stared at him as Javier continued to talk.

"It'd be gangster, Seeker. Plus, you get jumped out of your ghetto crew, then join up with us and take them out... that'd be hard. Make you look big time to all the bangers who have been down with Owen Street forever."

Javier was really trying to sell this to Seeker.

"It's a trap." Seeker told himself. "Maybe I do get to be even with Hector and those guys, then I'm in Owen Street. I'm a Hood; eventually a Creeper. Getting jumped out by them would probably be a lot worse than getting jumped out by the Little Killerz."

"Plus," Javier's expression changed and his eyes got angry. "It'll show how loyal you are to us."

"Look," Seeker started. "I don't want you to think I'm dissing you or anything..."

"Then don't." Javier interrupted. "You need us. Otherwise you got nothing."

"I just got out of the Little Killerz."

"They jumped you out. Beat your ass bad. They're gonna keep doing it." Javier was getting impatient.

"Maybe they will. I just don't want to be with anybody right now."

Javier stared at Seeker.

"Okay," His expression to Seeker was stern. "Have fun being dead."

Javier and the rest of the Owen Street Hoods walked away.

In case they were still watching him, Seeker acted like he was eating his lunch; unfazed.

It was tough.

He wanted to throw up.

Chapter 41.

As soon as the bell rang, Seeker left Cutter as quickly as he could. He also left from a different exit than he normally did.

He wanted to avoid Hector and anybody else in the Little Killerz. He also wanted to avoid Javier and the Owen Street Hoods.

Normally, he'd hang out with Hector and the others. Or hang out with Angel. Or he'd paint.

"I don't want to do anything." He thought. Seeker moved as quickly as he could down the street. Seeker went as fast as he could go without looking like he was running.

Even when he was really far away from the school, Seeker had his antennae up in case he saw any of his new enemies.

"Stay down, Seeker." He told himself. "Stay inside. Out of sight, out of mind. Let Hector, Javier, Angel and everybody else forget about you."

Seeker wanted to stay home from school but that would cause more problems. He'd get in trouble for missing, he'd fall behind in his schoolwork, and everybody would know he was hiding.

"I don't need to give them anymore reasons to think I'm a punk."

Chapter 42.

Seeker walked into his house and saw Mario sitting on the couch playing "Assassin's Creed." Seeker didn't even have to look at the TV. He could tell what game it was by the sounds coming from it.

"What's up?" Mario asked like it hadn't been many days since they last saw each other.

"Hey." Seeker said.

He went into his bedroom and dropped his backpack on the bed. Seeker thought about doing his homework but then realized he was hungry.

Seeker walked back out into the kitchen area. He looked in the refrigerator. He picked up a plastic butter cup that was filled with pasta from the night before. Seeker was glad that it was there. His sister was a good cook. Seeker was so hungry he thought he might eat the whole thing.

He put some of it on a plate. Then Seeker poured himself some juice. He walked toward his bedroom.

"You're not gonna heat that up?" Mario asked.

"Why do you care?" Seeker wanted to ask but didn't.

"Nah."

"You wanna play?" Mario motioned to other controller sitting by the couch.

"I gotta do my homework."

"Come on," Mario smiled. "One game. We never get to play together anymore."

"That's cause you're never here." Seeker said.

"Yeah..." Mario was still smiling. "So make the most of it right now. Come on Seeker!"

Seeker smiled. He put down his food and sat on the couch next to his brother-in-law.

A little over an hour later Seeker and Mario were watching "The Amazing Spider-Man" on DVD. Seeker liked the ones with Tobey Maguire and Kirsten Dunst better. He thought this new one was just okay.

Seeker loved the way Spider-Man moved around the city. If he could do that he could throw up tags in some really cool places. He'd never get caught. Seeker could also stay away from Hector and everybody else.

Seeker and Mario were having such a good time that he almost forgot about his problems. He'd polished off all the spaghetti in the butter cup.

"So, I gotta ask," Mario started. "Did you get the number?"

"What number?" Seeker was confused.

"Of the truck that ran over your face?" Mario cracked up after he said that.

"I fell down."

"You mean something fell on you!" Mario continued laughing. Seeker liked Mario. He didn't take anything too seriously.

"Yeah."

"Come on Sergio, what's the deal?" Mario wasn't laughing now. He seemed to really be interested in knowing what was up with him.

Seeker told Mario what was happening with Hector, Javier and Angel.

"Some people might say you blew it with that girl Angel." Mario said as he took a sip from a large soda he'd bought at the liquor store. "Not me."

"You don't think I'm weird?" Seeker ate some chips. "I could've totally got with her."

"You're not weird at all. The people that do think that... they're gonna be the ones that end up stuck."

"Like you are?" Seeker wanted to ask but didn't.

"You have a lot of time to do all those grown-up things. And let me tell you, when you're finally old enough to do half the things you want to do now, you'll see that either they were worth waiting for or they were no big deal at all."

"No big deal." Seeker thought.

"I wish everything with Hector and the others was no big deal." Seeker hoped he didn't sound like too much of a wimp to Mario. "If I could be invisible I would be set."

"Well Seeker," Mario started. "As bad as things may seem now you're free from all of that, right?"

"I guess."

"You are."

"How? I've got even more enemies?" Seeker couldn't make sense of what Mario was saying.

"So what."

"So what? I have a bunch of people that want to beat me up. It's never gonna end."

"It'll end." Mario laughed. "When you're your age you think that every terrible thing is gonna last forever. It doesn't. Nothing does. Even when you're an adult. You're a smart kid. You've got a lot going for you. You love painting; your sister says that you're doing really good in school..."

"None of that matters." Seeker interrupted.

"It matters. Trust me. You know what else? You're smart enough to not want to be in a gang anymore. Some people never get that smart. You're not even fourteen yet and you know better than to stay away from that."

"What does that matter if I'm dead?"

Mario stared at him. As if on cue, someone in "The Amazing Spider-Man" movie got killed. Mario looked at the screen for a moment and then looked back at Seeker.

"Well, you're dead if you stay in a situation that's gonna probably get you killed anyway, right?" He was talking about the Little Killerz.

Seeker didn't have anything to say. Mario was right.

Seeker knew that he had to get out of the Little Killerz at some point. He wasn't going to be in a gang his whole life. He couldn't be.

Seeker wanted to ask Mario why he wasn't home more. It was rare that they could sit and talk like this. Usually when Mario was home his kids were climbing all over him and his sister was talking to him about something.

The more Seeker thought about it, the more he realized that he really liked Mario. He thought he was good guy.

Seeker didn't want to start questioning Mario's life. Not to his face anyway. But one thought that he couldn't get out of his head was this:

"How could Mario give me such good advice about my life, yet his own life was mess?"

Seeker didn't ask Mario about that.

"Maybe when I'm older." He told himself.

Chapter 43.

Seeker's plan to stay under the radar seemed to work for a few days. He was so on edge that it was easy to keep his guard up.

"This won't last forever." He told himself. "None of those guys are gonna forget about this. They can make a bunch of mistakes. They can think I'm gonna be somewhere that I'm not. I go some place once that I shouldn't be... they catch me slipping even a little bit; I'm dead all over again."

Seeker would see Anthony, Irvin and Nathan around school. He knew that he didn't have to worry about them. Alone they were nothing.

When Hector came back... that's when Seeker's problems would really start. He was gonna be looking for Seeker all the time; just waiting for the right moment to start something.

"Maybe I should've taken Javier's offer?" He briefly thought.

Seeker knew that wasn't the answer. It would have protected him but eventually those guys would realize that Seeker wasn't down for Owen Street. He wasn't gonna jump anybody, do crimes, or any of the other things he knew they would ask him to do.

It was Thursday. Seeker figured he had one more day at Cutter and then Hector would be back on Monday.

He wished he could think of someway out of this. Some gangster move that would make him look like a hero and rid him of his problems with Hector, Angel and the Little Killerz forever.

Chapter 44.

"Sergio." It was Mr. Setari.

School was out.

Seeker was hoping to get leave campus like a ghost. It had worked well so far. He didn't want Mr. Setari slowing him down.

"Hey."

Seeker turned and walked backwards as Mr. Setari talked to him. He hoped that he would get the hint since he'd done that to him before when they talked.

"Sorry I didn't have time to rap with you the other day." Mr. Setari continued.

"It's cool."

"What'd you need?"

"Forget it."

"You serious?" Mr. Setari snapped angrily. He stopped following Seeker. Seeker stopped walking a little. He didn't expect Mr. Setari to get mad.

"It's no big deal." Seeker was trying to keep moving; for some reason he didn't feel like he could just walk away now.

"You know Sergio," Mr. Setari started. "I know you're grown up. I know you're cool now... but that doesn't mean that you stop being nice to somebody you used to know."

Seeker stopped walking completely.

"I can't talk to you."

"What?" Mr. Setari was confused.

"Just forget it."

"No Sergio, I'm not gonna forget it."

At that point Mr. Setari led Seeker behind a brick wall. It faced some windows that were part of the counselor's office. Students often hid there when they were supposed to be in class and Mr. Robert was looking for them.

"So what's up with you? When did you become a punk?" Mr. Setari was mad but he also didn't seem like he was talking to Seeker as a teacher. Seeker had a feeling he could say what was really on his mind and not get in trouble.

"Why are you calling me that?" Seeker was trying to be tough.

"Look around Sergio, there's nobody here. So you can stop with the act and be real with me. What's going on with you?"

Seeker stared directly into Mr. Setari's eyes.

He was overcome with emotion.

"Look at my face, Mr. Setari! This happened because of you!"

"What are you talking about?" Mr. Setari couldn't believe what he was hearing. "Just because you got in a fight with somebody..."

"This wasn't anybody!" Seeker yelled. He was over trying to contain himself. He'd been watching his every move and looking over his shoulder for too long. "This was my friends!"

"Why would your friends do this to you?"

"Don't you get it? We're a gang? They jumped me out. They beat me down and left me on the street like a dog. And now because of you I'm gonna be looking over my shoulder for the rest of my life."

"Why? What do I have to do with it?" Mr. Setari wasn't angry anymore. He was concerned.

"Remember that kid you busted?"

"Hector?"

"Yeah. He's my friend. Well, he was. He runs the Little Killerz. He was gonna get you back."

Seeker stopped short of telling him how. He may have been out of the Little Killerz but he was no narc.

"Don't worry, it's not gonna happen. Those guys saw me talking to you. They thought I told you what was up. So don't worry. I took a beating for you. They're not gonna mess with you any more... just me."

Mr. Setari stared at Seeker.

"He was really gonna try and get me for busting him?"

"Yes! You dissed him in front of everybody. Hector's crazy."

"Maybe there's something we can do? Maybe we can keep him from coming back to the school?"

"How?" Seeker asked. "He hasn't done anything? If you stop him from coming, he'll know it had something to do with me. It'll just make it worse. I'm alone now. I'm not in the Little Killerz. I'm not with anyone."

Seeker felt better after he let some of his feelings out. He knew this wasn't gonna change anything but at least it wasn't weighing on as much him anymore.

"Is there anything I can do?" Mr. Setari wanted to help Seeker. Seeker believed that. He just couldn't.

"Why'd you have to come to Cutter? Why couldn't you have just left the past in the past? I'm not a little kid anymore." Seeker knew what he was saying might hurt Mr. Setari. He just couldn't keep his feelings inside.

"I'm sorry, Sergio. But I'm here now, and you are too. If there's anything I can do to help you let me know."

"Thanks."

They stared at each other for a little while longer and then Seeker walked away.

Chapter 45.

Seeker was painting as quickly as he could. He wasn't nervous, he was just filled with so much energy and emotion that he had to put it someplace.

He was spraying the paint on so fast, it seemed like his name just appeared on the wall before him.

As he maneuvered the cans and switched up the colors, Seeker got a weird feeling inside.

"I have it." He thought.

He started to fill in the letters of his name.

S-e-e-k-e-R

Seeker had to be careful. If he messed up filling in the letters it wouldn't have the effect he wanted it to have. "It has to look like it it's coming out of the water." He kept telling himself over and over.

As sure as he was that he was going to achieve the effect he wanted, he knew that one false move could mess the whole thing up.

And then... as if he'd been able to do it the whole time, Seeker stepped back from his work and saw something that before this had only been in his mind.

Try as it might, the water on Seeker's painting couldn't stop his name from emerging out of it.

It couldn't be held down.

And Seeker wouldn't be held down.

He picked up the cans that still had paint in them, stuffed them into his backpack, pulled the hood of his hoodie down over his head and walked away.

Now he had to come up with another tag to put up all over town.

Chapter 46.

Seeker got up early that Friday. He ate, brushed his teeth and went to school. Seeker would've showered but he'd done that the night before.

He knew that his life was still full of problems, but getting that tag right had given him a new found confidence.

Seeker knew that he had a gift. He knew that if he worked really hard at it, he could do something with graffiti. He didn't know what; he just knew that he loved it.

It had been a rough time. He'd lost a lot of friends, his girlfriend, and he'd basically made himself a marked man with two gangs.

Still Seeker was optimistic.

"This is gonna end," He told himself on the way to school. "But I'm never gonna stop painting. Ever."

Seeker was walking really fast. He was almost at school. Despite his newfound optimism, Seeker wanted to get onto the school grounds where he knew he would be safe.

Seeker had been doing this for awhile. He was good at it now.

Hector would be back at school that Monday.

But that Friday morning he was standing half a mile down the street.

Waiting.

Chapter 47.

Some of the students who got out of out zero period early had snuck off campus.

"Hector's not supposed to be back until Monday." Seeker told himself. "Why's he so close to the school?"

Standing with Hector were Anthony, Irvin and Nathan. And Angel.

She had her arms around Hector's waist; just like she'd had them around Seeker's not too long ago.

"He can give you what you want." Seeker thought. "Just another person Angel can say she's been with."

Seeker would love to have turned around. He would have loved to have done anything but keep walking to school.

He knew he couldn't. Seeker didn't slow his pace at all. If he did anything that made it look like he didn't want to walk by them they would never let him forget it.

Cutter had a large field that Seeker was walking by. The gate that was attached to the fence was open. Seeker could have easily cut through that. He would have been on campus. If the Little Killerz came after him he could run and get help.

He took a deep breath and kept walking in the same direction.

"When they mess with me it's gonna be different this time." Seeker kept telling himself.

He tried to walk a little taller. Seeker wanted to make himself look a little more imposing.

As he got closer none of the Little Killerz moved toward him.

He continued walking.

Seeker was in front of them now. He thought he heard them saying something but he tried not to hear it.

"I'm almost passed them." He thought.

Seeker felt a rock hit his leg. It hurt.

Hector, who he assumed threw it, didn't throw it to hurt him. He just wanted to get Seeker's attention.

Seeker wanted to keep walking but he knew he couldn't.

He turned and faced them. Seeker was about fifteen feet away from the Little Killerz.

"That's it?" Seeker's tone and expression were stern. "That's the best you got? Throwing rocks?"

Hector didn't seem to know what to say. Irvin, Anthony and Nathan weren't going to say anything if he didn't.

Seeker could feel some of the other Cutter students gathering around.

"Maybe they'll help me?" He knew nobody would. Nobody wanted to face Hector.

Seeker had to.

"You guys are sorry." He said to his former gang.

Seeker turned and continued walking. He knew this wasn't over but he was gonna take any advantage he could get.

He saw that a bunch of students were watching them. There were at least 50 of them there.

"We're sorry? You're the one that doesn't like girls. Huh, Angel?" Hector said.

Angel just smiled as she hung on Hector.

"Hope you like my leftovers." Seeker countered.

He knew that he was gonna have to fight now. It was coming.

"Keep walking, punk!" Hector yelled. "You're probably gonna go tell that teacher you ghetto ass narc!!"

Seeker stopped walking and stared at Hector. He put down his backpack and stared at him. He wasn't as nervous as he thought he'd be.

"Lets go Hector," Seeker smiled. "Just you and me this time."

Hector walked away from Angel. He and Hector were standing a foot from each other now.

Hector didn't look as mean to Seeker now.

"Stay hard. Stay down." Seeker told himself.

"You want me bounced from school for good. That's what's gonna happen if I pop you first." Hector stated.

"Stop making excuses, Hector. You're not so tough without any back up."

Hector was fuming.

"Those punks can't help you." Seeker motioned to Anthony, Irvin and Nathan. "They'll follow you but they aren't gonna do anything. All you are is a punk, Hector. That's why I'm out of the Little Killerz. That's all any of you are."

Suddenly, Hector took a swing at Seeker. He ducked and charged Hector to the ground.

Seeker reigned down punches in him.

Seeker hit him with lefts and rights. Hector tried to cover up but Seeker didn't care. He was on top and he was throwing punches. He was worried that Anthony, Irvin and Nathan might try and grab him but he figured he could take them if they did.

Hector was strong. Even amidst Seeker's hailstorm of punches, Hector managed to crack him a few times in the face.

The punches were hard and Seeker could feel his nose starting to bleed.

"Keep hitting him!" Seeker told himself.

Hector's nose was bleeding and he had some blood coming down his cheek.

Hector used his legs and threw Seeker off of him. Seeker quickly got to his feet. He kicked Hector a bunch of times as he got up. It didn't stop Hector but it gave Seeker some distance.

Now they were standing across from each other again. Their arms were up in fighting positions.

Hector was battered but he was still ready to go. Seeker knew that it was gonna take a lot for him to beat Hector this way. Hector was a really good fighter. He'd beaten up people in high school who were way bigger than him.

Hector slugged Seeker in the face.

Seeker could feel some teeth in the back of his mouth loosen. He also tasted a lot of blood.

Hector cracked him again.

Seeker was getting dizzy. He had to hit Hector hard... somewhere. If he did that it would stop his momentum and Seeker could jump on him again.

Hector threw a few more punches that Seeker was able to block. He managed to hit Hector on the sides of his body, but he mostly hit his elbows and arms.

Then Hector slugged Seeker in the stomach; a few times. They were fighting in close now. Each of them digging in. Hector continued to get the better of him in these exchanges.

Seeker knew eventually Hector was gonna overpower him. He practically already had.

No matter what Seeker did, whether he was close or far away from Hector, it wasn't enough.

Then Hector grabbed Seeker and was about to throw him to the ground. Seeker felt himself falling backward.

"He can't take me to the ground." Seeker told himself. "If he does I'll never get up."

He had to do something. Seeker couldn't go down. Not until he had nothing left.

Seeker started throwing punches again. As many as he could, as hard as he could, hitting Hector's chest, arms, shoulders... and then Seeker punched Hector in the throat.

Seeker heard him gasp.

Hector stopped pushing Seeker to the ground.

Seeker seized this moment and grabbed Hector now.

With everything Seeker had he threw Hector to the ground.

Some of the students were yelling things but Seeker couldn't hear them. He didn't jump on Hector.

Seeker just wanted this fight to be over but he couldn't walk away.

He moved to kick Hector.

Out of nowhere... Principal Fry ran up.

Chapter 48.

All the students backed away a little bit when they saw Principal Fry. At the same time none of them of them wanted to miss what might happen next.

"Get away from him, Sergio!" Principal Fry yelled.

Seeker stood back. He'd never been happier to see a principal in all his life. He didn't even mind being called "Sergio."

He turned and looked at Anthony, Irvin and Nathan. They wouldn't look at him.

Then he eyed Angel. She was expressionless.

They had all sided with Hector. And now he was lying on the ground and would surely be in more trouble. The Little Killerz were leaderless now. Seeker would take his chances with them on the street.

Hector got up and tried to get away. Principal Fry grabbed him.

"Not so fast, Hector." Principal Fry said.

"Get off me! I'm not even in school." Hector tried to pull himself away from him. "Let go of me!"

Hector started cursing. Saying every bad word he could think of. None of the students could believe Hector had called Principal Fry those names.

He continued to try and get away from Principal Fry.

Then he tried to hit him in the face!

Principal Fry blocked it and wrapped his arms around Hector so he couldn't move.

Then Mr. Robert ran over. He easily took Hector away from Principal Fry. Hector knew better than to fight with Mr. Robert. He led him away.

Seeker relaxed for the first time in what seemed like forever.

"Lets go, Sergio." Principal Fry motioned for Seeker to start walking.

Seeker wasn't worried at all. He didn't care if he got suspended.

He was on his own now.

Seeker was free. Really free.

As he walked away he looked straight ahead. Eventually, he made eye contact with Javier. He was smiling. Seeker stared at him for a little while and looked away.

Chapter 49.

After Principal Fry got done talking with Hector, he had Seeker come into his office. He thought he might pass Hector as he went in. There was another door in Principal Fry's office. That was the door Hector was sent out of.

"I'll see Hector again but until I do I'm not gonna trip on it." Seeker told himself.

Seeker sat across from Principal Fry.

"What's been going on with you? You come to school all beat up? You get into a fight with Hector who I thought was your friend?" Principal Fry never took his eyes off of Seeker.

"I'm out of everything now." Seeker said. He wasn't gonna mention the Little Killerz. He wasn't gonna mention Angel. He knew that Principal Fry knew what was up.

"You can't fight all the time though. That's no solution."

"I had to fight Hector today. That's the last one, though. At least the last one that's gonna happen here."

"Well, I'm not gonna lecture you. You know the deal... I have to suspend you." Principal Fry said flatly.

Seeker knew it was coming. He'd been hanging out with Hector for a long time. Even though they'd gotten into their fair share of trouble together, Seeker had never been suspended.

"I understand. It won't happen again."

Principal Fry seemed confused. He hadn't expected Seeker to accept his punishment so easily.

"How long will I be suspended?" Even though he knew it was coming, Seeker wanted Principal Fry to know that he cared. That he wasn't taking it lightly.

"Well," Principal Fry eyed the calendar on his desk. "Today is Friday. I'm gonna bounce you until Wednesday."

Seeker nodded.

"This won't happen again." Seeker said. "I just want to do good, draw and paint, sir."

"I'm glad to hear that, Sergio. I just hope you mean it."

"I do." Seeker said.

And he did.

He was bummed about being suspended. About having his fight with Hector go on his record, but it was something that he had to do. It was worth it.

People could say a lot of things about Seeker, but he'd fought Hector and gotten suspended.

Seeker was down.

And right now, that was what mattered.

"I spoke with Mr. Setari," Principal Fry stated. "He told me what was going on. You're not gonna have to worry about Hector anymore. Not at this school anyway."

Chapter 50.

They called Seeker's house so that an adult could pick him up. The only person home was his sister.

The vice principal had to go to each class and get all of Seeker's assignments. He also went to his locker and brought Seeker all of his books.

"Like sister like brother," Mr. Robert smiled as Seeker and his sister walked to the parking lot. Mr. Robert was standing by the gate inside the school. He was holding a book. He liked to read in between classes when there weren't a ton of students around.

"I wonder if they make him do that?" Seeker thought. "To set a good example for us or something."

Seeker and his sister got in her car and drove out of the Cutter Middle School parking lot.

His sister didn't come down on Seeker at all for getting suspended. She just wanted to know what happened. Seeker told her but he made it a point to say he was never going to get suspended again.

"I know," She said. "I was surprised when I got the call. You've never been suspended before... and you hang out with some creeps."

"Not anymore." Seeker said.

Chapter 51.

Counting that Friday, Seeker had a total of five days off.

After two days, Seeker had completed all the coursework that the teachers had given him. He spent the rest of his time drawing, watching TV and playing video games.

Seeker thought about going out and painting but he hadn't come up with a new design for his name yet.

Sunday afternoon, after working on some sketches, he walked out into the living room and found his dad there watching TV.

"Hey." Seeker said as he went into the kitchen.

"Hi."

Some of the bruises had started to heal on his face from when the Little Killerz jumped him out. Seeker had brand new ones from his recent bout with Hector.

Seeker poured himself some juice and grabbed some chips. He walked back into his room.

"You should become a boxer." His dad said. He held up his fists.

Seeker was so startled that his dad was talking to him he didn't do anything but stare at him.

"You're fighting so much anyway."

"I got suspended." Seeker finally said.

His dad nodded his head.

"It's not gonna happen again." Seeker offered.

"You're not the first punk kid to say that." His dad laughed. "You don't think I said the same thing?"

"Yeah."

"You're a good artist, Sergio. I used to draw. I was good but you're better." His dad looked at the TV and then back at him.

"Really? What did you draw?"

"I wasn't drawing on walls like you. I took some classes at the junior college. I did that for awhile before your mom died."

This was the first time that Seeker ever remembered his dad talking about his mom. He was 7 when she died.

"Do you have anything I could see?" Seeker asked. He was genuinely interested in this man he didn't know.

"Somewhere."

And then, just like that, his dad went back to watching TV.

Seeker sat there for a moment and then slowly stood up. He started walking back into his room wondering if the man who had just appeared in the living room would ever come back.

"This whole time he's been watching me draw things. He knows I do graffiti art." Seeker thought; amazed.

"After my show is over we can look for some of my drawings if you want?" His dad never took his eyes off the TV screen.

"Yeah. Just call me. I'm gonna be in my room drawing."

Seeker went into his room and shut the door. He was so excited he wanted to bounce off the walls. Seeker didn't know what happened. He didn't know what had made his father start talking to him. He just hoped that this was gonna happen a lot more.

Chapter 52.

As Seeker was walking to school, he was thinking about some of the drawings his dad had shown him when he was suspended. They were mainly of buildings, or mountains, but Seeker liked the way looked. They were just pencil drawings but they looked real. Like the person drawing them had actually lived around what he was capturing. Seeker had an idea that he might use some of his dad's drawings in his next tag design.

Seeker and his dad had hung out a little bit each day he was suspended. The Tuesday before Seeker went back to school, they went for a drive so Seeker could show his father his tags.

He was a little nervous at first because he didn't know how his dad would take him doing something illegal.

As it turned out, his dad seemed to like Seeker's drawings. He'd even seen some of them before when he was driving around. That day together his dad just stared at them. The longer he stared the more Seeker got the impression that he had a lot of pride in his son.

"You really know how to use that spray paint, Sergio." He commented.

Seeker also found out a few more things about his dad that weekend. He had actually started going to college when he graduated high school. Then his mom got pregnant with his sister and he had to stop. Seeker also found out that his dad used to play guitar in a punk band. They played really fast versions of popular songs and the singer sang them in Spanish. Lastly, Seeker found out that when he was a baby, his parents had been renting a house, and not the small apartment that Seeker had always thought he'd lived in.

They didn't spend a ton of time together during Seeker's suspension, but compared to the past six years it felt like a lifetime.

Chapter 53.

"Turn off your cell phones! Keep them out of sight!" Mr. Robert yelled as Seeker walked into the school.

They made eye contact.

"Welcome back, Sergio. Try and stay back this time." Mr. Robert said in his matter-of-fact, booming voice.

"Okay." Seeker smiled.

He continued walking. Across the hallway Seeker saw Anthony, Irvin and Nathan. They hadn't seen him yet but he didn't care if they did.

"They're nothing without Hector." Seeker reminded himself.

He watched them talking to one another, looking around. They were still the Little Killerz but it wouldn't be long before Javier started leaning on them. They'd probably join up with Owen Street... and then they'd go after Hector.

Seeker stopped looking at them. He didn't want to think about that stuff. Seeker didn't have to anymore. And he was grateful.

He passed Angel and some of her girlfriends.

"She's so pretty." Seeker thought. Her long, black hair looked perfect. Angel was wearing white, short shorts and a tight, pink shirt.

Seeker would've kept staring but she was glaring at him now.

He knew that eventually when he was with a girl, it was gonna be more meaningful than it would've been with Angel.

Seeker continued moving. He took the sketchbook that Mr. Setari had given him out of his backpack. He made his way toward a planter. He couldn't wait to start sketching out his new ideas.

He sat down and got right to work. Seeker knew the bell was going to ring and he wanted to make his drawing time count.

And then, as if he was painting, he started making lines on the page. They weren't really anything yet, but eventually they would percolate into something. He was doing his best to recall the drawings his father had shown him.

Then Seeker made eye contact with Mr. Setari. He gave Seeker a slight smile and raised his head. Seeker smiled and gave him the peace sign.

Then he went back to drawing. Seeker was as free as he had ever been and it felt great.

The End

About the Author

Evan Jacobs was born in Long Island, New York and he moved to Irvine, California when he was 4 years old. He lived there for a year before relocating with his family to Fountain Valley, where he still lives. As a filmmaker, Evan has directed 12 low budget films and he's also had various screenplays produced and realized by other directors. He is currently hard at work on several movie and book projects. Evan also works for the Tustin Unified School District as a Behavior Interventionist in their Special Education department. "Down For His Crimes" is his fourth young adult novel. You can find out more about him at http://ronnisbooks.blogspot.com/.

19744400R00069

Made in the USA
Charleston, SC
09 June 2013